Also by Tom Decorte

DECORTE, T. (2000). *The Taming of Cocaine. Cocaine Use in European and American Cities.* Brussels, VUB University Press.

DECORTE, T. and KORF, D. (2004) (eds.). *European Studies on Drugs and Drug Policy.* Criminological Studies. Brussels, VUB University Press.

DECORTE, T. and SLOCK, S. (2005). *The Taming of Cocaine II: a 6-year Follow-up Study of 77 Cocaine and Crack Users.* Brussels, VUB University Press.

DECORTE, T., SCHEIRS, V., VANDER ELST, D. and MUYS, M. (2007). *Provisions for Amphetamine Type Stimulant Users in European Prisons.* Brussels, Cranstoun Drug services.

DECORTE, T., MORTELMANS, D., TIEBERGHIEN, J., DE MOOR, S. (2009). *Drug Use: an Overview of General Population Surveys in Europe.* Lisbon, European Monitoring Centre for Drugs and Drug Addiction (EMCDDA); Brussels, Belgian Science Policy Office.

DECORTE, T. and FOUNTAIN, J. (eds.) (2010). *Pleasure, Pain and Profit. European Perspectives on Drugs.* Lengerich, Pabst Science Publishers.

DECORTE, T., POTTER, G. and BOUCHARD, M. (2011). *World Wide Weed. Global Trends in Cannabis Cultivation and its Control.* London, Ashgate Publishers.

DECORTE, T., PAOLI, L., KERSTEN, L., HEYDE, J., VAN DUN, E. and VLAEMYNCK, M. (2014). *Cannabis Production in Belgium. Assessment of the Nature and Harms, and Implications for Priority Setting.* Ghent, Academia Press.

DE KOCK, Ch., DECORTE, T., VANDERPLASSCHEN, W., SCHAMP, J., DERLUYN, I., HAUSPIE, B., JACOBS, D., and SACCO, M. (2016). *Substance Use among People with a Migration Background: a Community Based Participatory Research Project.* Garant-Maklu, Apeldoorn / Antwerp.

DECORTE, T., DE GRAUWE, P. and TYTGAT, J. (2017). *Cannabis Sous Contrôle. Comment?* Brussels, Editions Racines.

REGULATING CANNABIS

A detailed scenario for a nonprofit Cannabis Market

TOM DECORTE

Archway Publishing books may be ordered through booksellers or by contacting:

Archway Publishing
1663 Liberty Drive
Bloomington, IN 47403
www.archwaypublishing.com
1 (888) 242-5904

ISBN: 978-1-4808-6143-5 (sc)
ISBN: 978-1-4808-6144-2 (e)

Library of Congress Control Number: 2018904354

Print information available on the last page.

Archway Publishing rev. date: 4/30/2018

For Kaat, Marie and Julia
For Maaike

CONTENTS

INTRODUCTION

Recent Developments in Cannabis Policy

1. The Americas: a Breakthrough in Conventional Cannabis Policy

In December 2013, Uruguay became the first country in the modern era to legalize cannabis, when president José Alberto "El pepe" Mujica signed a law to regulate recreational cannabis. In the United States, thirty states and the District of Columbia currently have laws broadly legalizing marijuana in some form. Starting with Oregon in 1973, individual states began to liberalize cannabis laws through decriminalization. In 1996, California was the first state to legalize medical cannabis, sparking a trend that spread across most other US states. In 2012, the vast majority of states allow for limited use of medical marijuana under certain circumstances. Some medical marijuana laws are broader than others, with types of medical conditions that allow for treatment varying from state to state. In 2013, Colorado and Washington became the first states to legalize cannabis for recreational use. In November 2014, cannabis regulation ballots were approved in the states of Oregon and Alaska. Today, eight states and the District of Columbia have adopted the most expansive laws legalizing marijuana for recreational use. California, Nevada, Maine and Massachusetts legalized recreational cannabis in 2016 through ballot measure. In Massachusetts, retail sales of cannabis are expected to start later this year in July. Voters in Maine similarly approved a ballot measure legalizing marijuana in 2016. Most recently, sales of recreational-use marijuana in California kicked off on January 1ˢᵗ, 2018, although the state has not yet adopted rules for licensed marijuana growers or retailers, nor has it begun accepting licenses.

In 2013, the Canadian government introduced sweeping legislation designed to permit the recreational use of marijuana throughout the country by July 2018, fulfilling an election promise by Prime Minister Justin Trudeau. The bill, inspired in part by the experiences of cannabis regimes in Colorado and Washington state, goes well beyond the U.S. situation, where marijuana remains prohibited at the federal level. In Canada, the federal government will change criminal law nationally and will license growers and set product standards while leaving it up to the provinces to handle distribution and manage retail sale.

Clearly, a breakthrough in conventional cannabis policy is emerging. The current policy trend towards legal regulation of the cannabis market is increasingly seen as a more promising model for protecting people's health and safety and has changed the drug policy landscape and the terms of the debate. The prohibitive model has failed to show any sustained impact in reducing the market, while imposing heavy burdens upon criminal justice systems; producing profoundly negative social and public health impacts; and creating criminal markets supporting organized crime, violence and corruption.

2. Meanwhile in Europe: Inertia at the National Level versus New Ideas Bottom Up

But while in the Americas cannabis policy reform is taking off, European nations seem to be lagging behind, at least at the level of national governments who seem to be in denial of the changing policy landscape. Tom Blickman, a senior project officer at Transnational Institute (TNI) in Amsterdam, monitors these trends meticulously, together with his colleagues: "Cannabis policy reform falls under the remit of European Union member states, not under the competence of the European Union (EU). However, European law builds on the three UN drug control conventions that oblige member states to adopt measures to establish recreational cannabis as punishable (penal or administrative) offences, leaving very few options for reform other than non-enforcement of infractions. Moreover, EU member states have agreed to cooperate and to take the most appropriate measures against cannabis cultivation for recreational use.

At the local level, however, disenchantment with the current cannabis regime gives rise to new ideas. In several countries in Europe, local and regional authorities are looking at regulation, either pressured by grassroots movements – in particular the *cannabis social clubs* (CSCs) – or due to the involvement of criminal groups and public disorder." In the Netherlands, municipalities signed a Joint Manifest in which they asked the government to allow for space to regulate the supply of *coffeeshops* currently not allowed. In late 2017, the newly formed coalition announced that they would seek to implement an experimental new system in certain cities where coffeeshops could legally acquire weed from a state-appointed producer. In Copenhagen (Denmark), in Mons (Belgium) and in Berlin, Frankfurt-am-Main, Hamburg and Cologne (Germany), local authorities promote *coffeeshop*-like dispensaries with a regulated supply. In Spain and Switzerland, regional and local authorities want to allow cannabis social clubs, while in Belgium, Portugal, France and the UK, campaigns for CSCs are gaining momentum.

As in the United States, different policies regarding personal use and possession for personal use already exist in Europe, from *de jure* decriminalization in Portugal and the Czech Republic to full prohibition in Sweden, as well as intermediate *de facto* decriminalization in countries such as the Netherlands, Belgium, Luxembourg, Switzerland, Germany and Spain. However, to extend this model to regulate cultivation practices, is not self-evident. The current legal and political straitjacket in Europe is extremely difficult to reconcile with the request of local authorities to effectively regulate the supply of cannabis for recreational use as an alternative to the negative consequences of the current restrictive arrangements. It would mean that European states would have to violate the UN conventions, just as Uruguay, Canada and the federal U.S. government have done. This is not impossible, but will require political will to do so.

3. Legalization: a Binary Choice Between Prohibition and Commercialization?

Many of the U.S. states which have legalized cannabis have adopted profit-driven markets which resemble those for alcohol. This is despite a considerable public health literature documenting how alcohol and tobacco companies maximize profits by targeting young and heavy users, spend heavily on advertising and promotion to normalize use, downplay the health risks of their products, and actively lobby regulators and politicians for industry friendly regulatory environments. Highly profitable alcohol companies simply have more money to spend on lobbying politicians and regulators, resisting restrictive regulation, and influencing the public than public health groups. There appears to be little reason to believe a profit-driven commercial market for cannabis would be any different. For example, cannabis businesses in Colorado have formed the National Cannabis Industry Association (NCIA) (consisting of nearly 1,000 cannabis businesses) to promote their interests, and cannabis industry representatives are on the working group considering appropriate regulation of the cannabis sector for the state. In another parallel, the cannabis industry's media has referred to daily cannabis users as the "backbone of the industry." The advertising regulations for the cannabis market in Colorado have been modelled on the voluntary code of conduct developed by the alcohol industry, and the Colorado cannabis industry has attempted to weaken pesticide regulations for cannabis cultivation.

Jonathan Caulkins, an American drug policy researcher at Carnegie Mellon University in Pittsburgh, has repeatedly pointed out that legalization is often falsely framed as being a binary choice between prohibition and some regulated commercial model, such as govern alcohol in much of the world. For their part, drug policy researchers have pointed out that there are actually many more regulatory options for legal cannabis markets than alcohol style regulation, including "social clubs," "grow-your-own," "not-for-profit" and government monopoly. These "in-between"-models could be safe and feasible options for policymakers to move a meaningful distance along the spectrum towards legally regulated cannabis markets without crossing over to full commercial availability. Yet these options are often not developed in any detail or adapted to a specific jurisdiction, reducing the likelihood they will be taken seriously by policymakers tasked with developing new regulatory regimes for cannabis.

Jonathan Caulkins is quite right to argue that, when prohibition is rejected, a fundamental question is what kinds of organizations should be granted the right to produce and distribute the formerly prohibited good? Allowing a commercial market is just one of many architectures for legalization, one at the far end of a broad spectrum of options. Moving directly from prohibition to commercial legalization leaps from one extreme to the other, bypassing other, safer forms of legalization, including the non-profit model. Furthermore, it is an irreversible leap, says Jonathan Caulkins: "Once created, a multi-billion dollar industry will use its clout to lobby for self-preservation and more. Entrepreneurs from the industry already occupy many seats on Oregon's recreational marijuana rules advisory committee, and there are real concerns that the tobacco industry will expand into the cannabis product space after national legalization. Welcoming free-market dynamism makes sense for most products. Private industry invents new product forms, drives down costs, and markets aggressively to expand consumption. Those are boons when consumers can be trusted to make prudent decisions concerning the purchase and use of those goods."

Yet, it is important to note that cannabis is also consumed by people with a substance use disorder, and by daily and near-daily users. Obviously, most people who use cannabis are entirely happy with that consumption. But the smaller number of problem users consume far more and more often. From the suppliers' perspective, a daily user is as profitable as almost 15 occasional users, according to Jonathan Caulkins. Problem use is a major driver of sales and profits. If we want to undercut the black market without promoting greater problem use, a commercial market with profit-driven companies definitely has more disadvantages compared to a market with not-for-profit corporations, or a co-op or "cannabis club model".

4. This Book's Objective

In Belgium, a similar development as described above, has been observed. On the one hand the national government is in denial of the changing cannabis policy landscape elsewhere and it seems to suffer from inertia in acting upon calls for change from local authorities and grassroots movements. These local authorities are confronted with a range of problems that, in the end, cannot be solved without some kind of a regulated and transparent supply chain of recreational cannabis.

In November 2013, I published an academic vision statement together with two academics from other disciplines (Professor Paul De Grauwe, an economist, and Professor Jan Tytgat, a toxicologist) to stimulate the cannabis reform debate in Belgium. We presented a critical evaluation of the Belgian cannabis policy. The Belgian cannabis policy is based on honorable objectives, but it did not succeed in realizing its major goals – a decline in the number of cannabis consumers, and particularly the number of individuals with cannabis-related problems, a decrease in the physical and psychosocial damage caused by cannabis abuse or misuse, and a drop in the number of negative consequences of the cannabis phenomenon for society (public nuisance among other things) – over the past decades. The government expenditure on fruitless repressive strategies that aim to reduce supply, is substantial. This expenditure displaces more cost-efficient investments based on scientific evidence about effective prevention, about the reduction of demand and about harm reduction. In our vision statement of 2013, we argued that the policy option for a regulated cannabis market is a serious one that should be studied as careful as the continuation or intensification of the current policy.

In a second attempt in 2016 to fuel the debate on cannabis policy reform, we launched a concrete and detailed scenario for a regulated cannabis market. This books summarizes the proposal, which aimed to initiate a wide social, political and academic discussion in Belgium. Given the fact that the prohibitionist approach imposed on cannabis by the international drug control system still persists in many countries around the world, while at the same time local and regional authorities – sometimes pressured by grassroots movements - are advocating change, I believe the scenario we elaborated contains a relevant contribution to the debates elsewhere in the world. In many countries around the world, cannabis policy reform is still pending, or has been inadequate, and I hope this book contributes to a new genre of publications that think about how best to design and implement approaches to legalization.

Much remains uncertain about cannabis legalization. For instance, it remains entirely unclear how legalization-induced increases in cannabis use will affect use and abuse of alcohol and tobacco. Advocates hope cannabis will substitute for alcohol, thereby reducing the myriad problems caused by alcohol abuse. Pessimists fear that greater cannabis use and dependence will translate into greater tobacco smoking and alcohol abuse. No one knows for sure; even if we had perfect studies concerning substitution and complementarity in the past for fluctuations in supply while cannabis remains prohibited, the relationships could be different in the long-run after full legalization at the national level. Since the scale of alcohol and tobacco-related death and harm are so enormous compared to cannabis-specific outcomes, just this one (among many) key uncertainty makes it impossible to know today whether we will celebrate or rue legalization in decades to come. That strongly suggests implementing legalization slowly and by stages. That is why my central argument with this book is that for governments that decide to reject prohibition – and there are many legitimate reasons to do so – the most fundamental question is what kinds of players should be granted the right to produce and distribute cannabis. My argument would be: start with a market restricted to not-for-profits, or even just cannabis clubs and co-ops that sell to members only. After a decade, if few problems are detected, then the right to produce could be extended to other kinds of organizations. The scenario I present in this book provides one concrete example of what the first step of such a staged approach might look like. Obviously, with the input of drug experts from all relevant sectors and disciplines, the scenario presented here can be refined and adapted to the local context of a particular country, and at least form the basis for a debate about possible regulation models. We can imagine many variants.

5. This Book's Structure

In **Chapter 1**, I provide a description of the Belgian drug policy and the most important recent trends and debates around cannabis in my own country. Obviously, as explained above, the Belgian drug policy is not the focus of this book at all. The principal aim of this book is to present a detailed and concrete scenario for the development of a non-profit-driven legal cannabis market, and to contribute to the current debates elsewhere in the world on how best to design and implement approaches to legalization of cannabis. Before diving into the details of the scenario presented in the following chapters, it seems appropriate to provide at least some elementary background information about the context in which this scenario was developed.

In **Chapter 2,** I summarize a few important reasons why regulation of the cannabis market is a serious option. Then I present the major points that form the foundation of the concrete scenario for a regulated cannabis market. I describe the principal objectives and principles of the proposal presented in this book.

In **Chapter 3**, I present the scenario in detail. First I argue that there should be a preparatory phase before the whole implementation process, in which: (1) the scenario is worked out in detail; (2) an information campaign is launched, through which citizens are fully informed about the objectives and modalities concerning regulation; (3) preparatory scientific research is conducted if necessary. In any process of cannabis policy reform it is very important to preserve the balance between the (urgent) implementation of a new policy and the risks of an overhastily introduced policy. This is why I argue for a cautious scenario, in two phases (**see figure 1**). In a first phase, three legally regulated channels can be created. A first pillar is regulation of the cultivation and possession of cannabis for strict personal use ("home growing"). A second cornerstone of the proposed model is the cannabis social club(s). These clubs are not-for-profit associations that operate as a private club for cannabis users, who collectively grow cannabis in order to provide for the personal consumption of the members. The third pillar is the supply of medicinal cannabis to particular groups of patients, for medical use only.

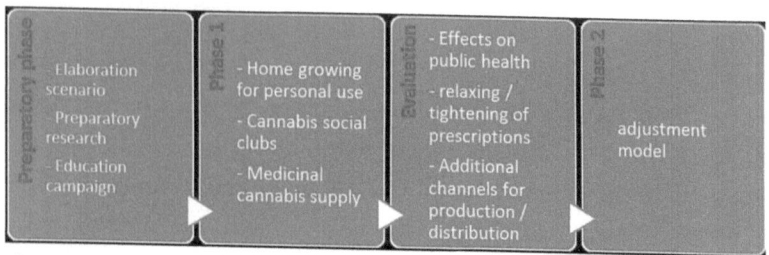

Figure 1: A Cautious Scenario for a Regulated and Not-For-Profit Cannabis Market, in Two Phases.

In **Chapter 4**, I elaborate the second phase – after a serious evaluation of the implementation of the model and its effects on numerous parameters, the model can be adjusted if necessary: it must be verified which parts of the new regulation should become less or more strict, and if additional channels for cannabis production and distribution can be created or not.

Finally, I discuss some necessary preconditions for the implementation of the scenario in **Chapter 5**.

The draft of this scenario is based on scientific findings from the international literature. In particular, the publications of the Transform Drug Policy Foundation (particularly the guide *How to regulate cannabis. A practical guide,* 2013) were valuable sources of inspiration. These manuals list the major challenges, scientific findings and different options concerning regulation. In this book, I try to construct a scenario on the basis of the scholarly literature that takes into account the specific context and the way the cannabis market manifests itself in many countries nowadays. To improve the readability of this document, I did not use an academic reference style as often seen in academic journals or monographs, but I mention all the sources I've used at the end of this book.

CHAPTER 1

The Background: Belgian Drug Policy and Recent Trends and Debates on Cannabis

Cannabis policy in Belgium is not the focus of this book at all. In the following chapters, I want to present a detailed and concrete scenario for the development of a non-profit-driven, legal cannabis market, and in doing so, I hope to contribute to the current debates elsewhere in the world on how best to design and implement approaches to legalization of cannabis. Having said this, it seems appropriate to provide at least some background information about the national context in which this scenario was developed, before diving into the details of the scenario presented in the following chapters. That is why I provide in this chapter a description of the Belgian drug policy and the most important recent trends and debates around cannabis in my own country.

1. The Belgian Legal and Drug Policy Framework on Cannabis

The first Belgian narcotics law dates from February 24, 1921, and has since been amended by two laws in 2003 and several royal decrees and ministerial circular letters. These changes to the Narcotic Drug Law of 1921 were implementations of the drug policy as set out by the Federal Drug Policy Note of 2001. This document—which was largely based on the recommendations of a parliamentary commission on drugs (1997)—provided a framework for the juridical-technical debates and reforms of the Belgian drug law in 2003 and 2004. The 2001 Federal Drug Policy Note takes a "normalizing" stance and considers drug use to be a social reality. According to this policy note, drug use should primarily be considered as a problem of public health rather than belonging to the criminal sphere.

The 2001 Federal Drug Policy Note created the framework for an *integral and integrated drug policy*. This means that drug use is seen as a multidimensional problem (socioeconomic, health, crime) that accordingly requires a multidimensional approach wherein all relevant sectors (prevention, repression, treatment, harm reduction) should play their parts. Due to the complex state structure of Belgium, the framework consequently implied that all policy levels (federal, regional, local) and sectors are involved with their particular competences. The main priorities of the Belgian government were to reduce the number of drug users, to reduce the physical and mental effects related to drug use, and to reduce negative consequences such as public nuisance and crime in society. Accordingly, the current Belgian drug policy is built on three pillars: (1) prevention of drug consumption; (2) harm reduction, treatment, and reintegration; and (3) repression as an option *ultimum remedium*.

With the translation of the Federal Policy Note into law, cannabis received a separate "status" from other illegal drugs (such as cocaine, heroin, ecstasy, speed, etc.). Furthermore, the law provided a distinction between (1) minors (under eighteen years old according to Belgian law); (2) adults who use or possess illegal drugs; and (3) adults who use or possess cannabis. For minors, the possession and use of any illegal drug is prohibited without exceptions. For adults, the possession of a small amount of cannabis (maximum three grams or one female plant) for personal use has the "lowest prosecution priority." In practice, this means that law enforcement will only draft a simplified police report. However, this can only be the case when aggravating circumstances are absent—such as the involvement of minors, being part of an organization linked to drug trafficking, problematic use, causing physical injuries to others, or causing public nuisance. If any of these aggravating circumstances are applicable, the police will make a regular police report and inform the public prosecutor. These cases are punishable by a fine or incarceration. Lastly, the possession of other illegal drugs remains prohibited for adults.

From a legal perspective, cannabis still is an illegal substance in Belgium. Its possession, use, distribution, and trafficking can be subject to criminal or administrative sanctions. Moreover, since the federal elections in 2014, the new government opted for a return to a zero-tolerance drug policy. The political parties in power agreed that the existing "tolerance" for cannabis was a problem, and in their governmental agreement it was stated that "the possession of drugs is forbidden. The use of drugs in public space cannot be the subject of any tolerance policy" (Federal Government 2014, 92).

2. Belgian Framework for Medicinal Cannabis

In Belgium, the supply and possession of herbal cannabis for medicinal purposes is prohibited. Non-pharmaceutical products based on cannabis and cannabis derivatives (e.g., cannabis oil, tincture) are not allowed either. Only licensed pharmaceutical medicines based on cannabis were made available in 2015 in Belgium.

In June 2015, a royal decree came into force that regulates products that contain tetrahydrocannabinol (THC). This royal decree formally prohibits the distribution of the cannabis plant for medicinal usage. Until now, the only cannabinoid-based medicine that has obtained a license to be sold in Belgium, is Sativex, a cannabinoid oral spray. Sativex can only be used as a treatment for spasticity caused by multiple sclerosis, and it can only be used by patients for which other treatments have been proven to be ineffective. In addition, there must be a significant clinical improvement regarding spasticity in a first test phase. A patient can only receive reimbursement when this medicine is prescribed by a neurologist and obtained from a hospital pharmacy. Any Belgian physician has the "therapeutic freedom" to prescribe Sativex, but when physicians who are not neurologists prescribe the medicine for patients who do not suffer from spasticity due to MS (e.g., for chronic pain), the treatment will not be reimbursed.

Cannabis products containing solely cannabidiol (CBD) and no tetrahydrocannabinol (THC) cannot be sold in Belgium as therapeutic agents. Until now, there have been no CBD products that have obtained a license from the Federal Agency for Medicines and Health Products (FAMPH) to be sold as regulated medicines.

Belgian patients who do not suffer from MS are forced to rely on illegal sources of cannabis, including home cultivation, web stores, street circuits, social supply, Dutch *coffeeshops*, and Dutch pharmacies. The cultivation of cannabis in Belgium is formally prohibited; this also applies to cannabis cultivated for medicinal or scientific purposes. Belgium has signed the 1961 UN Single Convention on Narcotic Drugs. Countries that want to legally regulate cannabis cultivation have to create a special office that is responsible for the production of cannabis for medical or scientific purposes—the Dutch Office of Medicinal Cannabis (OMC) is an example of such a government office. Until now, no such office has been established in Belgium, and there seems to be no legal initiative for setting up such a framework in the near future.

In practice, Belgian residents with serious medical ailments other than MS do have a particular option to obtain medicinal cannabis products of pharmaceutical quality, but this implies breaking the law. Since physicians in Belgium have "therapy freedom," they are not in violation when they prescribe unlicensed medicines for their patients, such as medicinal cannabis. The Belgian law on healthcare professions states that practitioners cannot be subject to regulatory limitations in the choice of the means used, either for making a diagnosis, for setting up a treatment and its execution, or for the execution of magisterial preparations. This means that any physician in Belgium is allowed to prescribe medicinal cannabis for any possible indication, but on his or her own responsibility and with the consent of the patient. With this prescription, Belgian patients can go to pharmacies in the Netherlands that sell medicinal cannabis produced by Bedrocan, the only company in that country that is licensed to produce medicinal cannabis.

Buying cannabis in a Dutch pharmacy is the only way that customers are guaranteed safe and standardized cannabis. Furthermore, by doing so, the patients' treatments are supervised by physicians. However, transporting medicinal cannabis from the Netherlands to Belgium remains an illegal activity, which means that they risk prosecution for import of illegal drugs when they cross the border between the Netherlands and Belgium. Moreover, most Belgian patients do not live close to the Dutch border. For them it is a long journey to the Netherlands. Those people have a choice: either they can buy a larger amount of cannabis to ensure a supply for a longer period (but at the same they risk a more severe punishment when caught), or they can choose to buy a small amount (but then they have to travel more often to the Netherlands). For people who are suffering from severe medical problems, neither of these options is ideal.

Some law proposals have been submitted to the Belgian parliament, but any attempt to create a broader legal framework for medicinal cannabis products has been unsuccessful.

3. A Particular Phenomenon: Cannabis Social Clubs in Belgium

The cannabis social club (CSC or "club") model has been present in Belgium for over a decade now, as the first CSC was established in 2006. The emergence of the model in the country follows the issue of the 2005 ministerial guidelines, which attributed the lowest priority for prosecution of instances concerning the possession of one cannabis plant or three grams of cannabis—in the absence of aggravating circumstances or public disorder (as I described earlier). The initiators of this first CSC argued that by imposing a limit of *one plant per member*, the cannabis club would respect the threshold established by the ministerial guidelines. They assumed cannabis clubs would thus also be considered as a "low priority" for law enforcement. The other CSCs that were created subsequently have followed the same reasoning, and thus the principle of "one plant per member" became central to the functioning of Belgian CSCs (as further described below).

As opposed to the cannabis clubs in Uruguay—which form one of the legally regulated supply channels for recreational cannabis users—a regulatory framework for these CSCs has never been created in Belgium, leaving the CSCs in a rather vulnerable position. Many CSCs in Belgium have been the target of police interventions, with their crops being confiscated by the police, and have faced criminal lawsuits. To some extent, this explains the volatility that has characterized the presence of the model in Belgium since 2006, with CSCs closing down and new ones appearing. Circa February 2014, I identified 5 active CSCs, with the model being represented in both Flanders and Wallonia. A more recent study by my colleague Mafalda Pardal offers an overview of the changes in the Belgian CSC landscape since its inception and found that only two of the previously active CSCs remain operational today. A total of seven active CSCs, and five inactive CSCs were identified by her. In comparison to other settings where the model is active (in particular Uruguay and Spain), the number of Belgian CSCs remains relatively small.

The CSCs remain up until today the result of grassroots efforts within the drug user movement. Some of the CSC activists have in fact also been involved in other local drug user groups and organizations, and had closely followed the earlier emergence and development of the CSC model in Spain. The relations among the

Belgian CSC activists are not always characterized by collaboration, and there seem to be factions or cliques among them. Perhaps in part due to that lack of trust among the various CSC representatives, no supra-level organization such as a CSC Federation (which exists for instance in Spain and in the United Kingdom) have been created.

Beyond that, according to a recent account, the Belgian CSCs have also engaged with other organizations in the broader cannabis movement, including grow shops and seed banks in Belgium and abroad, as well as cannabis testing labs or providers of such testing kits. The Belgian CSCs are also aware of and have contacts with CSCs in other countries, and have also enrolled in other national, regional or European lobbying or advocacy organizations, such as the European Coalition for Just and Effective Drug Policies (ENCOD) or the Dutch Alliance for the Abolition of Cannabis Prohibition (VOC).

The emergence and development of the CSC model (and movement) in Belgium has gathered some media attention. The CSCs have communicated about their goals and activities through that channel, thus reaching a broader audience. However, the coverage of the CSC model in the domestic print media has tended to focus primarily on criminal justice issues affecting the CSCs which could result in negative representation. Belgian policy makers have shown limited involvement in discussing the model (at least through the media), which may suggest that an actual debate about this supply model has not fully been initiated yet.

The Belgian CSCs have typically been formalized as nonprofit organizations in the national registry for this type of associations. In their bylaws, the CSCs have explicitly introduced the supply of cannabis as a goal, often with reference to the principle of one plant per member. Access to these organizations and thus access to the cannabis produced by them is only open to members, who must also fulfil specific requirements. Candidate members typically must be eighteen or twenty-one years old, Belgian residents or national, and declare already having used cannabis prior to their enrolment at the CSC. Different criteria may apply for individuals using cannabis for medical reasons seeking to join a CSC (for instance, such users may be asked to produce a medical prescription or recommendation letter).

The cannabis supplied by the Belgian CSCs is produced by some of the members of each of the organizations, which typically receive a compensation for the cannabis grown. The cannabis produced is then delivered by the CSCs either at so-called "exchange fairs", i.e., collective gatherings where the CSC members who have previously ordered cannabis from their CSC come together to collect it; or directly at the CSC, at the member's home or in a location previously agreed upon between the CSC and the member. Regular and independent toxicological testing of the cannabis produced by the Belgian CSCs is difficult and expensive, and thus remains a weak point of the model as it exists in Belgium.

While these constitute typical practices of the Belgian CSCs, I should note that there is certainly diversity in terms of the functioning of these organizations, and that multiple variants of a CSC model may actually co-exist in the country.

Most Belgian CSCs have at, some point in time, experienced legal problems following police interventions. Some of those cases are still under investigation or a verdict by the courts at stake has not yet been made. However, some of the concluded cases have had important implications for the further development of the model to date. On the one hand, the two cases involving the first Belgian CSC, which resulted in a favorable result for that club may have had a positive impact to the emergence of new CSCs in the country. The charges brought in the first of the two cases related to possession of cannabis and participation in a criminal organization. While initially condemned, when the case was brought to the Court of

Appeal, that Court was unable to pass judgement as the criminal prosecution had become time-barred.

The second court case involving that CSC came about in the sequence of two public demonstrations organized by the CSC (during which some CSC representatives planted cannabis seeds in pots), but the defendants were acquitted. This CSC has currently been subject to a new police intervention, with some of its representatives being held in custody for a few weeks. So far, there has also been one documented case of a "shadow CSC" in Belgium, which has also been brought to court. In that case, the "CSC" was found to have many more plants than the number of members, and the operation was described as a façade for actual sales of cannabis.

One other CSC has been charged for both possession of cannabis and for facilitating the use of cannabis – with the decision of the Court of Appeal convicting the CSC representatives for the first offence, but acquitting for the second. In another process involving this CSC, the public prosecutor asked for the formal dissolution of the organization as its bylaws explicitly mentioned a goal (and activities) which constituted a criminal fact (i.e., the cultivation and distribution of cannabis). This was, to my knowledge, the first case where the issue was raised, and may have implications for the future of the model in the country. That CSC has since then changed its bylaws, removing the controversial paragraphs, and has suspended the cultivation and distribution of cannabis among its members.

A recent press release by the Belgian College of Public Prosecutors refuted the interpretation of the 2005 Ministerial Guidelines often brought forward by the CSCs and activists to justify the legitimacy (and legality) of their activities, making the stance of that body more clear – and which could represent a more repressive approach towards the remaining CSCs active in the country.

A final observation relates to *medicinal cannabis social clubs*. In

Belgium, two cannabis social clubs have installed formal arrangements adapted to medicinal cannabis users' needs. One club has
a separate sub-unit for medicinal users, the other club exclusively
serves medicinal users. These structural arrangements for medicinal members include reduced prices of cannabis strains as well
as flexibility in relation to frequency of distribution and quantity
distributed to medicinal members. The membership criteria of
both clubs are more strict as compared to other CSCs: users who
wish to enroll at the medical unit or at the medical cannabis social
club need to present a medical certificate or prescription. The other
cannabis social clubs in Belgium allow medicinal cannabis users as
well, but they do not provide particular services to them.

4. Recent Debates on Cannabis Regulation

Belgium has faced mounting calls from academia, civil society and
professionals for comprehensive reform of the drug policy, and the
cannabis policy in particular. I already referred to the academic
vision statement I published with two colleagues in 2013, in which
we critically questioned Belgium's cannabis policy. A year later, two
other well-known and influential criminologists (Brice De Ruyver
and Cyrille Fijnaut) published a book called *"The third way. A plea
for a balanced cannabis policy"*. One of the premises by these authors
was that a strict, controlled and limited form of cannabis regulation
can be incorporated within a (possibly reformed) framework of
United Nations and European legislation. Both scholars argued that
cultivation of cannabis for personal consumption, cannabis social
clubs and the distribution of medicinal cannabis to specific groups
of patients could be regulated.

   In 2016, the detailed scenario for a regulated nonprofit cannabis
market presented in this book was published in a Dutch and French
version (Belgium has three official languages – Dutch, French and
German – but French is used by 33% of the population and Dutch or

Flemish is used by more than 60% of the population). Most recently, an interdisciplinary working group at the Catholic University of Leuven has composed a working group that aims to bring together existing scholarship and scientific expertise on cannabis policy. The recommendations of this working group (consisting of 15 professors from different academic disciplines) were presented in March 2018, and called for a fundamental reform of the country's cannabis policy.

These claims for a policy reform were also picked up by various professionals in the drugs field. The three main organizations that coordinate and represent all treatment and prevention centers specialized in alcohol and drug problems in Flanders, Wallonia and Brussels have issued vision statements on cannabis policy. These three associations advocate for a reform of the country's cannabis policy. Public health considerations should be the primary rationale of our cannabis policy, not repressive strategies. A new approach in cannabis policy should aim at an effective reduction of health risks; while the current criminalization stigmatizes cannabis users and impairs their well-being. The Walloon and Brussels organizations advocate even more explicitly for a regulated model of cannabis supply.

A remarkable new "player" in the debate is Peter Muyshondt, a deputy chief of police. As a drug warrior, he had been thrown into a moral conflict after his brother died of a drug overdose nine years ago. Losing his brother to drugs changed him from a drug warrior to an advocate of legally regulating and controlling drugs. He published two books (in 2015 and 2017), and became the face of the campaign "Anyone's Child: Families for Safer Drug Control" in Belgium.

Civil society advocates have also entered the debate. In June 2016, the two oldest Belgian cannabis social clubs joined efforts in developing a "Blueprint for the regulation of cannabis in Belgium". The proposal included three different legal channels for the supply of cannabis: home growing, cannabis social clubs and supply for medical reasons via pharmacies. In 2017, a civil society movement – STOP1921 – was formed to campaign for a reform of the Belgian drug policy. The name of the initiative refers to the year 1921, when the first penal law on drugs in Belgium was voted, and the foundations for a repressive policy for the next century were created. The movement consists of individual citizens and dozens of organizations that want to push the political actors to take action.

Meanwhile, the Belgian political world seems to be in denial of the changing international policy landscape and of the calls for policy reform from academia, professional stakeholders and civil society. Youth sections of the green, socialist and liberal political parties – which can proclaim and communicate their own political agenda towards the party – explicitly plead for the legalization and regulation of cannabis, both in Flanders and in Wallonia. The youth department of the Christian party in Wallonia also advocates for regulating the cannabis market; the Flemish section rejects the idea.

Some of the mother parties – especially in the green, socialist and communist political families - endorse the idea of drug policy reform and regulation of cannabis. The socialist party in Wallonia is the most explicit: the Walloon *Parti Socialiste* (PS) advocates cannabis regulation (they submitted a law proposal in December 2017) and they would like to set up a cannabis social club in the city of Mons as a scientific experiment (I mentioned earlier several similar attempts in other European cities). However, the political parties that hold power in the Belgian government, the Christian-democrats, the liberals and the nationalist-conservative parties have written a zero-tolerance policy into their government agreement in 2014. Current official policy declarations are limited to a statement such as "We merely apply the law and principles as described in our government agreement."

More importantly, after more than 80 years of socialist local governments in the large city of Antwerp, the Flemish nationalists are now the most powerful party in the local city council since 2013. The mayor – and party leader of the Flemish nationalist and conservative party – is an avid ideologically inspired opponent of cannabis regulation, who wants to send a clear message that illegal drugs are dangerous and criminal. This political party has reinvented the "war on drugs" in Antwerp, resulting in a marked increase of police capacity in local drug teams, more arrests and fines for drug dealers and users, treatment programs as alternative sentencing trajectories, and more confiscated drugs. At the same time, the city has witnessed a spectacular increase in shooting incidents and violent retaliations. Most recently, another dimension was added to the debate: the role of organized crime in cocaine trafficking in the Antwerp port (considered to be one of the major hubs for cocaine trafficking in Europe), and how to tackle it. The last few years, the "war on drugs" in Antwerp has become a "national" topic, in the sense that it frequently features in columns, newspapers and documentaries. In the face of local elections in 2018 and federal elections in 2019, the controversy between advocates of drug policy reform and supporters of the repressive "war on drugs" might become an election issue. At the time of writing this book, I cannot predict whether cannabis policy in Belgium will remain stuck in a status quo, or evolve into a nationwide war on drugs, or in a process of drug policy reform.

Regardless of the fact whether or not Belgian cannabis policy will evolve, and if so in which sense, I am quite confident that similar debates are being held in many other countries around the world. On the one hand, local contexts, actors and factors may differ from one another, but on the other hand, it is true that there is a similar disenchantment with the current cannabis regime in many countries. In the next chapter, I offer some arguments for a reconsideration of prohibitionist cannabis policies.

CHAPTER 2

Cannabis Regulation: What It Is, What It Is Not, and Why We Need to Consider It

There are many reasons and arguments to claim that regulation of the cannabis market is a serious option. Any reader who is familiar with the issue of cannabis policy reform, will find nothing new in this chapter. For other readers, I use this chapter to briefly present some of the main arguments. Then I describe the principal objectives and principles of the detailed scenario for a regulated cannabis market presented in the third chapter of this book.

1. Why Regulation Is a Serious Option

The main goals of cannabis policies in most countries and jurisdictions can be summarized as follows: (1) a reduction in the number of dependent citizens; (2) a decrease in the physical and psychosocial damage caused by abuse of cannabis; (3) a drop in the number of negative consequences of the cannabis phenomenon (public nuisance and criminality).

Until today, most governments opt for an integrated approach in which prevention, treatment and repression are combined. With regard to the supply of cannabis, national governments invest in a repressive policy in regard to criminal organizations who have strong ties with cannabis trade. Criminal law and enforcement efforts of the police and justice system are the spearheads of most cannabis policies around the world today.

After decades of mainly repressive cannabis policies, it is time for a critical evaluation of the outcome of the enforced measures. In most countries, the available figures clearly indicate that repressive cannabis policies have not led to a decline in cannabis use in these societies and that the number of people who struggle with cannabis abuse or dependence appears to have increased.

A policy attempting to limit the supply of cannabis with repression is faced with a fundamental paradox. The more intense the repression is, and the better it succeeds in limiting supply and creating scarcity, the higher the price will be for the consumer and consequently the profitability of the production and distribution of cannabis. The high profits have a great attraction for (millions of) people who want to take risks, for "have-nots" who have nothing to lose or for people who are not afraid of crime or violence. The more intense the repressive approach, the more people dive into the production and distribution of drugs. This paradox has a number of important effects.

First of all, repressive cannabis policies quickly face their limitations. The fact is that the efficiency of this approach is limited by definition, because of the unstoppable increase in willing producers and distributors. This way, many illegal channels arise which governments can hardly control. Given the supply of drugs is extraordinary profitable thanks to its illegality, the suppliers have extensive financial resources with which they can hide their activities in a way that is becoming more and more sophisticated, or with which they can escape repression by bribery and corruption.

Repressive cannabis policies cannot significantly influence the supply of cannabis or the access to cannabis for users, let alone reduce it. They only lead to geographical shifts and transformations of the phenomenon. In practice, an intensified repressive approach applied to every drug user and everywhere is not feasible, due to budgetary limitations and the necessity to fight other criminal phenomena. The result is often a form of selectivity in the policy towards nuisance and in detection, prosecution and punishment.

The major consequence of the paradox is that it is an incentive for crime. The supply often occurs illegally and attracts a great number of suppliers competing intensely with each other. The illegal environment is bound to become a criminal environment. The harsher the law enforcement in practice, the more the illegal market is characterized by systemic violence (so-called "rip-offs", shootings, and so on) and the more "criminal" it becomes. The increased risk of arrest puts off small-scale grower hobbyists and only the professional criminal operators remain. The cannabis ban also leads indirectly to corruption, money laundering operations, and damage to other economic sectors. On an international scale, it leads to violent conflicts, drug money used for the arms trade, financing of terrorism and war, threat to democratic institutions and ecological damage.

Another consequence is that it is not possible to control the composition, the purity, the potency and the quality of illegal cannabis in general. The current Dutch or Belgian marihuana contains much higher concentrations of THC than 30 or 40 years ago, but that is just a consequence of the repressive policy. Growers preferably grow the strongest possible cannabis varieties as a result of the risk of getting caught.

Moreover, cannabis is grown in uncontrollable circumstances nowadays: it may contain harmful fungi, bacteria, pesticides or other contaminants (heavy metals, glass particles, and so on). In this context, we can only try to warn people when encountering critical danger ("early warning"), but we cannot take action. Besides, governments do not have the ability to restrict or influence the marketing strategies of the cannabis producers, as they do with the legal drug industries. If we compare a few things with alcohol and tobacco, a more consistent attitude of the government concerning the quality, the quantity and the labelling of cannabis is at least advisable.

In many countries, the amount of spending related to repression (i.e., the expenses for the detection and settlement of violations of the drug legislation by the police and justice system) is much higher compared to the public expenditure on prevention and treatment. This huge expenditure goes hand in hand with fruitless strategies that aim to reduce supply, and with a confinement policy. This expenditure displaces more cost-efficient investments based on scientific evidence on effective prevention, on demand reduction and on harm reduction. In my view, government expenditure must be spent on activities which clearly contribute to the realization of the major policy objectives. We cannot continue to carry on with symbolic investments.

2. Basic Principles for a Regulated Model

Repressive cannabis policies have failed to realize their major goals during the past decades. In my opinion, a regulated cannabis market offers the possibility to reduce the substantial government expenditure that goes hand in hand with the confinement policy and with the fruitless fight against the black market. At the same time, we can make more cost-efficient investments based on scientific evidence about the reduction of demand and about harm reduction. The major objectives of the policy in the scenario I present in the next chapter, remain: (1) a reduction in the number of citizens that use cannabis in a problematic way (and the reinforcement of the social norm of non-use); (2) a reduction in the physical and psychosocial damage caused by drug abuse; and (3) a decrease in the negative consequences of the drug phenomenon for society (among which public nuisance). In the long term, the cannabis policy has to lead – as has been achieved with the tobacco policy - to a decrease of the general prevalence of cannabis use and the postponement of the first use of cannabis (in other words: an increase in the age when someone experiments for the first time with cannabis).

2.1. Objectives of a Regulation of the Cannabis Market

A successful policy is a strategy that actually succeeds in controlling the risks of drug use as much as possible and at the same time strictly advises against the use of psychoactive drugs. A regulated market aims to:

- control all aspects of the *production of cannabis*;
- control the *way cannabis products are available*;
- pursue a *price-conscious policy* concerning cannabis products;
- control the *sales outlets of cannabis*;
- increase the controls on *the users and the locations* where cannabis can be used.

Additional objectives of the proposed reform of the cannabis policy include:

- the provision of *legal supply channels*, so that the cannabis user does not have to get involved with criminal environments;
- the reduction of illegal channels, the *weakening and in the long term the elimination of the black market* in cannabis and the deprivation of an important source of income for organized criminals, and in doing so taking away their economic power;
- the possibility of controlling the composition, the purity, the potency and the quality of cannabis in a general sense, for the *protection of public health*;
- the control of *marketing strategies of cannabis producers*, as we also do with legal drug industries (e.g., tobacco);

- the *reduction of the caseload in the law enforcement system* by reducing the number of cannabis-related cases that have to be detected and judged;
- the *reduction of the prison population* by reducing the number of people that are imprisoned for cannabis-related crimes;
- the *reduction of selectivity* in the approach to public nuisance and the detection of cannabis-related offences;
- the *fight against environmental pollution* caused by large-scale illegal cannabis production (cannabis plantations);
- the promotion of more cost-efficient investments based on scientific evidence about *effective prevention, about the reduction of demand and about harm reduction;*
- making *the job of prevention workers and social workers* easier by making their target audience more easily accessible and increasing budgets for education, harm reduction and treatment.

2.2. The Option for Stricter Regulation

There is a large spectrum of legal and political models available to regulate the production, the supply and the use of cannabis (or other narcotics) **(see figure 2)**. At the one end of the spectrum is situated the criminal market, which is created because of a complete ban. Next, there are less punitive ban systems: models with a partial/de facto/nearly legal supply, legally regulated market models with different restriction levels. At the other end of the spectrum are located the legal and commercial free markets.

Both extremes of the spectrum are completely non-regulated markets. The scenario I will present in the next chapter is based on the assumption that the two extreme options are connected with unacceptably high social and healthcare costs, because those who want to control the market (whether it is legal or illegal) are almost exclusively driven by profit maximization. The options in the middle offer the possibility to strictly regulate various aspects of the market, so that the potential adverse consequences of cannabis use and of the cannabis market can be kept to a minimum and the potential advantages can be maximized.

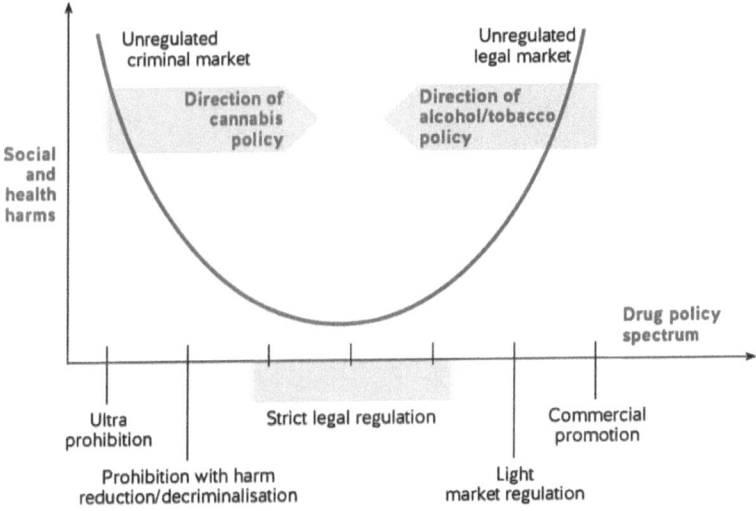

Figure 2: A Spectrum of the Possible Policy Options. Source: Transform (2007). After the War on Drugs. Tools for the Debate, p. 19. Transform Drug Policy Foundation, Bristol.

We should deliberately opt for a restrictive model, with a far-reaching form of government control and strict regulation. This kind of model is adaptable: when serious and careful evaluations are positive, it can be adapted in a later phase to a less restrictive and interventionistic model (if new social norms and social control mechanisms will be developed around the legal cannabis market). From a pragmatic and a policy perspective, this is a better scenario than the opposite scenario in which one has to retroactively introduce more restrictive controls because the market was not regulated enough. Our experience with the retroactive regulation of the tobacco and alcohol markets also taught us a lot, for that matter.

Additionally, the adaptable character of the model also works for the opposite direction. If independent and scientific evaluations show that certain regulations and provisions have to be formulated more rigidly, in that sense, the model can be refined. And if – during a later phase – other players are admitted to the cannabis market (for instance, independent farmers or commercial companies), the proposed model with all its restrictions and regulations can be used unabridged for the additional legal channels.

2.3. Regulation: What It Is and What It Is Not

Regulation of the cannabis market is – for sure – not inspired by a *laissez-faire attitude*. Proponents in the debate about regulation adhere to the repressive model obstinately out of the fear that the transformation of a *war on drugs* into regulation will lead to "free drugs for everyone". Or they polarize determinedly the societal debate by arguing that there are only two possible attitudes: those who "want to do something about it (by using repression)" and those who "gave up the fight.". However, the debate concerning "legalization" is only about regulating the phenomenon in another way.

Even though the terms "legalization" and "regulation" are inextricably bound up with each other, it is useful to make a clear distinction between these two. *Legalization* is merely a process of legalizing something presently illegal. *Legal regulation*, on the other hand, is the final product of that process and refers to a whole set of rules that control the product or behavior in question. If possible, I consciously avoid the term legalization, because some people misinterpret every proposal concerning legalization as a plea for some kind of commercial, unregulated free market. I do not agree with that idea at all. Basically, I plead for the creation of legal channels (thus a legalization), with a far-reaching form of stringent regulation.

Although regulation of drugs is often conceived as a

"liberalization" or a "weakening" of legislation, in fact it is the oppo-site: the point is to fit the drug production and distribution into a legal framework, so *strict controls* can be applied. Strict control cannot be applied under a total cannabis ban. Regulation enables government to control which drugs can be sold, who can get access to them and where they can be sold. Criminals can decide this if there is a total ban. Everyone can buy every kind of drug as long as criminals control the trade. Drug dealers don't ask for your identity card.

Another term that sometimes causes confusion is *decriminal-ization*. Decriminalization generally means: the abolition of the penalization of certain behavior. In some countries, the possession of (a small quantity of) cannabis for personal use, has been decrim-inalized. If this behavior is no longer punished or prosecuted, but not removed from the criminal law, we call this a *decriminalization de facto*. I need to point out here that decriminalization de facto here only refers to the *possession* of (a small amount of) cannabis and thus not to the *production* and *distribution* of cannabis. My proposal for a regulated cannabis market in this book concerns a *decriminalization de jure*: apart from the penalization for cannabis possession, the pe-nalization for certain forms of cannabis *production* and *distribution* will be abolished and replaced by legally regulated channels.

Regulating does not necessarily mean "commercializing". Nor does it mean the approval or promotion of intoxicant use, or the minimization of the dangers and risks of drug use. Besides, norms and lines are drawn by regulation. Every scenario of regulation cer-tainly abolishes the (administrative or criminal) sanctions for pro-duction, supply and possession of cannabis that take place within the parameters of the legal framework. However, all activities be-yond the legal framework (such as selling cannabis to minors, driv-ing a vehicle under the influence of cannabis), remain punishable. Criminal norms and sanctions are used for: (1) producers, distribu-tors or users who don't stick to the rules; (2) non-licensed producers and distributors who continue to produce merely for money.

I want to emphasize beforehand that legal regulation is *no silver bullet* or panacea for the drug problem. Regulation will not "solve" all problematic or harmful cannabis use. A cannabis ban doesn't lead to a drug-free world; a regulated model cannot create a risk- or damage-free world. Legal regulation aims to reduce or exclude the damage resulting from prohibition or criminal markets.

Another frequently occurring criticism is that a form of regulation will never help to dissolve the black market completely. It is correct to a certain extent: experience with tobacco showed that the illegal trade in cigarettes hasn't disappeared completely and this can be explained partially because of important differences between countries concerning tax regimes (so differences in price) for tobacco products. But even if the black market does not disappear completely, there still would be – from a global perspective - a decline in the black market (and its inherent criminality). Regulation will also end ineffective criminal law-enforcement tactics that keep on pushing the drug production and drug trade to other areas, without eliminating them (the so-called waterbed effect). By ending the cannabis ban, more resources become available to deal with the remaining illegal channels and other forms of criminality. Besides, this challenge will get a lot easier because by cutting off the illegal drug profits of criminals, their power will also shrink.

2.4. Seeking the Right Balance

The reform of a cannabis policy and the development of a detailed blueprint for a regulated market is an exceptionally delicate balancing exercise for various reasons.

First, the *international and juridical context* has to be taken into account. The perception that the war against drugs is lost once and for all, will not come via the big transnational organizations and bureaucracies. An important change in discourse through international treaties will not happen in the near future, because unanimous consensus is necessary in this area, and because a number of traditional exceptionally repressive-minded countries can be obstructive in complicated procedures. Moreover, international organizations – such as the United Nations (by means of the activities of the *International Narcotics Control Board*), but similarly the European action plans – aim for a uniform and stringent approach towards the drug phenomenon. But changes in the local and national policy will enfeeble the basic assumptions for the war against drugs. Meanwhile, many countries understand this. More and more countries, regions and cities are testing the flexibility of the international treaties. They do not want to wait longer for when and how the international treaties and agreements will be reformed, they want to develop as soon as possible a policy that enables them to get a grip on the phenomenon and its problematic sides. From a legal perspective, it is easy to argue that the international treaties allow regulation, on condition that the policy of other countries won't get a spanner thrown in their wheels.

A lot has been written about how national governments have the flexibility under international law to regulate cannabis production and trade for the purpose of recreational cannabis use. In 2014, a professor of criminal and procedural law, Piet Hein van Kempen, and a university teacher, Masha Fedorova, from the Radboud University of Nijmegen, concluded that legalization from the *internal perspective* of the current UN drug treaties (the Single Convention and the Convention against Illicit Traffic) is not possible. But in a second study in 2016 they examined the issue from the *external perspective* of human rights treaties (the International Covenant on Economic, Social and Cultural Rights, the European Social Charter, the International Covenant on Civil and Political Rights, and the European Convention on Human Rights). From this perspective, there seems to be a possibility for regulated legalization of cannabis production and trade for the purpose of the recreational user market.

Pleas for a regulated cannabis production and trade for the purpose of recreational use are often based on arguments connected with individual health and public health, the safety of citizens and the fight against criminality. The intent of this argument is that these interests can be protected more efficiently with the regulated cannabis model than with a prohibitive approach. That is interesting with regard to human rights because affairs of health, safety and crime fighting fall within the scope of that. So-called positive obligations for states arise from the right to health, the right to live, the right against inhuman treatment and the right to privacy. States have to take action to guarantee the fundamental rights of individuals. In this case it is about obligations to actively promote the individual's health and the public's health, and to actively protect the life, the physical and psychological integrity and the private life of citizens. Van Kempen and Fedorova (2016) concluded that the regulated approval of cannabis production and trade for recreational use can rely on positive obligations arising from international human rights treaties because of interests of individual health and public health, safety and crime prevention. According to international law, these positive human rights obligations take priority over the obligations from the UN drug treaties in cases where these conflict with each other. As far as there is the above-mentioned support, states also have by international law enough room to introduce that approval, despite their obligations to the drug treaties.

Nevertheless, a regulated model has to meet some essential conditions:

1   Relevant Importance for Human Rights

First of all, the regulated approval of cannabis production and trade has to protect the interests that are relevant proceeding from positive human rights obligations. In the debate about regulation of cannabis production, various arguments in favor of regulation

come up that find support in one or more of these positive obligations. These relevant arguments include that regulated approval
is advisable, because a regulation of this kind will lead to a better
realization of the following interests: quality control of cannabis;
control of the cannabis chain; reduction of peripheral criminality;
protection of the health, the life and the physical and psychological
integrity of neighbors; health protection for young people; decrease
in public nuisance and damage that leads to direct limitation in the
enjoyment of private life; and separation of the soft drugs market
and the hard drugs market (which could put up a barrier against
simultaneous availability and accessibility of soft drugs and hard
drugs). It is argued that regulation of cannabis production and trade
for recreational use applies under such circumstances as a positive
obligation to the protection of human rights. Support for this regulation is offered by the right to health (as defined in the International
Covenant on Economic, Social and Cultural Rights (ICESCR) and
the European Social Charter (ESC)) and the rights concerning life,
inhuman treatment and private life (as adopted in the International
Covenant on Civil and Political Rights (ICCPR) and the European
Convention on Human Rights (ECHR)).

2 Making a Reasonable Case for More Effective Human Rights Protection

The state has to make a reasonable case for regulation, in the sense
that it will realize the relevant positive human rights obligations
(concerning health, life, physical and psychological integrity and
private life) more efficiently than an approach in which production
and trade is prohibited. First, the regulated approval of cannabis
production and trade for recreational use has to provide more effective and better human rights protection than a cannabis policy
which is in accordance with the drug treaties (*demand for higher
effectivity*). Second, if a state wants to introduce a regulatory model,
it will have to make a reasonable case that it will lead to more

effective human rights protection than a prohibitive and repressive approach (*demand for plausibility*). Another question is whether a state that wants to regulate cannabis can immediately introduce it on a national level, or whether it should evaluate the effects through pilots and experiments. It is up to the state to consider if pilots are useful and if their deployment is advisable.

3   Basis and National Democratic Decision-Making

The judgement about whether state regulation of cannabis leads to more effective protection of human rights should be the result of democratic decision-making procedures.

4   No Disadvantage for Foreign Countries: Closed System

If a state allows a regulatory framework for cannabis production and trade for the recreational user market, then the control over this system must be to the extent that other countries suffer no negative effects from it, especially concerning exports from the regulating state. The protection of the interests of other countries must be guaranteed – and must preferably be even more effective – than operating within a prohibitive policy in accordance with the drug treaties. Thus a state must provide a nationally-closed system for production, distribution and maybe for use.

5   Obligatory Policy of Discouragement

If a state choses to regulate cannabis production and trade, the state has to provide for an adequate policy of discouragement, limitation and risk awareness of recreational cannabis use. This is not only necessary to create the most adequate assurance of human rights protection with the cannabis policy, but there is also an obligation in accordance with the right to health. By implementing this policy of dissuasion, the state will have to see what eventually is the most effective. Furthermore, it is important that obligations do not have to be implemented in such a way that they are counterproductive.

When designing a regulated cannabis model, these considerations must be taken into account. A first phase must provide for a number of reforms that can be implemented within the parameters of the current international treaties, such as the decriminalization of possession for personal use, the cultivation for personal use and cannabis social clubs. These measures are relatively easy to implement and are well-founded on the basis of the present *evidence base*. In addition to this, these measures may illustrate the political intention of a government to reform the international legal framework. In a later phase, a government can create additional legal channels (and for instance allowing licensed companies), if it is willing to negotiate around the existing barriers in the current international law or if the international legal context evolves.

Second, by reforming the cannabis policy there has to be found an important balance between the (urgent) implementation of a new policy and the *risks of an overhastily introduced policy*. Experiences with regulating alcohol and tobacco and the developments in the American states Colorado and Washington, teach us that the rash introduction of a regulation, in which one must introduce retroactively more restrictive controls because the market was not regulated enough, is a less desirable scenario. That is why I argue for a cautious and, at the start, very restrictive and governmentally-interventionist scenario.

Third, the development of an adequate regulated cannabis model is also a search for a design that on the one hand doesn't include *too many restrictions*, so that people continue to supply themselves through a parallel illegal market, and on the other hand a design that doesn't include *too few restrictions*, to make sure cannabis use and sale is not encouraged. There is and there always will be a tension between commercial interests (that are involved with maximizing profit, and thus tend to encourage and promote cannabis use) and the interest of public health (which is aimed at minimizing the damage and the risks, and thus at moderating and reducing cannabis use). It is my personal conviction that it is important to invest as much as possible in the protection of public health and to eliminate wherever possible the incentives for profit maximization.

2.5. Lessons from the Past

Of course there are various regulatory models for drugs that now-adays are not criminalized, or in other words "legalized" (nicotine, alcohol, caffeine and a great number of pharmaceutical products). These models show important differences depending on the product (the regimes for alcohol and nicotine are very different and have been developed over time). The production and distribution of alcohol, nicotine and medical drugs (legal substances) are mainly regulated by a free-market principle. These models excellently illustrate how a government with a legislative armamentarium (by which production, distribution and use don't have to be completely criminalized) can impose rules: quality norms, age limits for users, laws against intoxication in public, limitations concerning advertising and marketing, obligations concerning packaging and instruction leaflets, a smoking ban in public spaces and so on.

On the other hand, the experience with these models has shown that *commercializing substances* can have unintended and undesirable consequences. If government regulations are insufficiently restrictive and allow production of risky products through the mechanism of the free market (and thus by the principle of profit maximization), some dangers will come to the surface:

- For decades, the *tobacco industry* has tried to minimize the dangers for health and the risk of dependence of nicotine use. It remained silent as much as possible about its search for additives that could stimulate the absorption of nicotine. Tobacco companies could invest enormous amounts in scientific research that benefitted their interests, and at the same time keep under wraps the funded research that didn't please them.

- The *alcohol industry* invests millions of dollars in the development and design of new (alcohol) products that help increase alcohol consumption, sometimes with specific target groups (the "breezers", the "alcopops" ...). If governments want to introduce measures for dealing with problematic alcohol use, alcohol industry lobbyists lobby as hard and as long as they can to eliminate all measures that aim to reduce availability (e.g., a ban on so-called *happy hours*, an increase of the age limits, a ban on sale in slot machines, night shops, petrol stations and so on).

- The same mechanisms are at play with *pharmaceutical multinationals*. Displeasing scientific research is sometimes silenced in order for medicines to find their way to the pharmacies. Independently sponsored tests lead to a positive result in fewer cases; when pharmaceutical companies sponsor the investigation, the number of "positive" outcomes increases spectacularly. Through think tanks, supporting patient associations, seducing and deploying scientists, and by the organization or sponsoring of conferences, working visits and seminars, they defend their interests. This lobbying work serves to place certain disorders more prominently on the agenda, to influence the demand for a particular pharmaceutical product, to influence the prescription attitude of physicians, and of course to sell more branded medicines.

Briefly, the regulatory frameworks for tobacco (nicotine), alcohol and medicines can offer a lot of inspiration for a debate about the regulation of cannabis. At the same time, these models teach us a lot about the pernicious consequences of "commercialization" (a model in which profit maximization for producers is the major motive).

In the course of the past decades, cannabis has also been subjected to experiments concerning decriminalization and regulation that have been prepared and conducted on the national, regional and local level: The *coffeeshop model* in the Netherlands, and the *cannabis social clubs* in Spain and Belgium. Many countries have introduced some kind of variant of the so-called *Alaska model*: a system in which individual citizens or households have the right to grow a maximum amount of plants by themselves (in other words: a legalization of small-scale home growing). The models of decriminalization of 25 countries are described in the 2016 report *"A quiet revolution: drug decriminalization across the globe"* (including Argentina, Armenia, Australia, Chile, Colombia, Costa Rica, Ecuador, Estonia, Germany, Italy, Jamaica, Croatia, Mexico, Paraguay, Peru, Poland, Russia, Spain, Czech Republic and Switzerland).

In 2001, *Portugal* decided to remove the possession for personal use of all illegal drugs from the criminal law and to classify it under administrative law. Someone who is found in the possession of a small amount of drugs has to check in with a multidisciplinary compound board, some kind of a deterrence commission, in accordance with the new regulation. A majority of the population in the American states of Alaska, Colorado, Oregon and Washington voted, in a referendum, in favor of a regulation of the cultivation, delivery and sale of cannabis. Canada announced that it will regulate cannabis in 2018. Furthermore, there are 25 American states that introduced *medical marijuana programs* in the course of the past 15 years. Other countries also have a legally-regulated model for medicinal cannabis (including Canada, Chile, Finland, Great

Britain, Israel, the Netherlands, Austria, Spain and Czech Republic). Uruguay (a country that also signed the international treaties!) was the first in the world to regulate the entire production chain of marijuana in 2014. Each one of these regulatory experiments and systems can teach us a thing or two for future experiments concerning the legalization of cannabis.

We can learn from the mistakes concerning alcohol and to-bacco control, and from the experiments with decriminalization or regulation of cannabis elsewhere. The current prevalence of alcohol and tobacco use is the result of many decades of commercial pro-motion, often in barely-regulated markets. Considering the fact that cannabis still is illegal, we can proceed from a *tabula rasa*. We can start from the beginning by setting up optimal regulatory frame-works, in which all aspects of the market will be controlled. The experiments with the regulation of cannabis in foreign countries illustrate that the cannabis market does not have to function on the basis of commercial principles. There are other options, whereby public bodies or nonprofit organizations are managing the drug chain in a way to get rid of the financial incentives that initiate or stimulate drug use.

2.6. There's a Hefty Price to Pay

Opponents of a regulated cannabis market often argue that reg-ulation would be too expensive, both in terms of application of the new legislation and in terms of health costs as a result of the increase in cannabis use. Of course there will be costs bound up with the change to a regulation model, but they will be particu-larly small in comparison with the costs of enforcing the cannabis ban. Regulation not only saves a lot of money by no longer waging a useless and counterproductive drug war, but it also allows the generation of revenue by means of taxes (**see Chapter 5**). Under a cannabis ban, the limited present resources will be spent on counterproductive enforcement of the drug laws, to the detriment of expenditure upon proven health interventions. All income generated by legally-regulated cannabis sales can support health interventions, such as drug prevention, treatment and harm reduction initiatives. Even if cannabis use increases, the health damage and financial costs will decrease, and this generates a net profit for the society on the whole.

CHAPTER 3

A Regulated Nonprofit Model for Cannabis

In this chapter, I present a detailed model for a non-profit-driven cannabis market. It is a hypothetical scenario, which means it does not reflect the actual cannabis policy in Belgium, the country where I live and work, at all. It is also important to note that the model can be considered as "work in progress". If authorities decide to reject prohibition, and to take the path of a regulated cannabis market, the scenario presented here definitely needs refinement (more detailed regulatory regimes) and adaption to the local context.

I first point at the necessity of a preparatory phase as part of the implementation of the new model. I have repeatedly argued in the previous chapters that reforming a cannabis policy implies looking for a delicate balance between the (urgent) implementation of a new policy and the risks of an overhastily introduced policy. This is why I argue for a cautious scenario, in which initially three channels for cannabis supply are created: the cultivation and possession of cannabis for strict personal use ("home growing"), the cannabis social clubs, and the supply of medicinal cannabis to particular groups of patients, for medical use only.

1. Preparatory Phase

I already emphasized **in Chapter 2** that the implementation of a regulated cannabis model should be implemented cautiously and not necessarily in a hasty manner. There should be a preparatory phase before the whole implementation process, in which: (1) the whole scenario is worked out in detail; (2) an information campaign is launched, through which citizens are fully informed about the objectives and modalities concerning regulation; (3) preparatory scientific research is conducted if necessary.

The further *elaboration of detailed regulation* takes time and requires the input of field experts and drug experts from many disciplines. The model I propose in this book can undoubtedly be polished and refined. From a pragmatic and political point of view, it is important to sufficiently think about the restrictions that have to be built in, and about the necessary preconditions before the implementation of a new policy model. If the initial governmental regulations are insufficiently restrictive and allow for the production of risky products by the mechanism of the free market (and thus by the principle of profit maximization), then the retroactive introduction of more restrictive controls is a difficult matter. That is an important lesson from the experiences with alcohol and tobacco. Both the alcohol and tobacco industries have always firmly resisted measures aimed at supply reduction.

An adage in communication studies states that if political actors formulate a policy, they should provide *complete, timely, actual and consistent information*. If this is not the case, every citizen will interpret the policy in his or her own way. The possibility that the policy objectives will not be realized is much bigger in that case. If authorities communicate in a clumsy way about a cannabis policy reform, this may lead to great confusion about what will be legal and what will remain illegal among young people and among relevant actors in the field (police officers, magistrates, educators and teachers, social workers and so on).

It is very important to set up a *solid and well-considered education campaign* before the actual implementation of a new regulatory framework. The government must explain in a comprehensible and well-substantiated way what the underlying ideas of the new policy are, what the major principles of the new system are (so also:

what is legally allowed and what not!), what the role will be of the various actors and what rules will be applied in the transitional phase to the implementation (between the announcement and the actual implementation). In doing so, the government avoids great confusion amongst cannabis users and the major actors in the field.

It is also not unthinkable that authorities need to order *additional scientific studies* in order to profoundly dig out certain aspects of the regulated model. I think about, for example, the elaboration of a numerical scale in which the potency and the THC/CBD ratios of different cannabis products are indicated (**see Section 2.2.8**), a study of the most advisable price-fixing of different cannabis products and the related tax measures (on the basis of the experience with price-fixing and the tax policy concerning tobacco and alcohol products) or a study of the advantages and risks of *vaporizer*-appliances and *e-joint* devices and the labelling and standardizing of these devices.

2. A Legally Regulated Cannabis Model

Let us now turn to the proposed scenario itself. I propose a model, with three legally regulated channels : (1) *home growing for strict personal use*; (2) *cannabis social clubs*; and (3) *supply of medicinal cannabis* (**see figure 3**). After a serious evaluation of the implementation of the model and its effects on numerous parameters, the model can be adjusted if necessary (**see Chapter 4**).

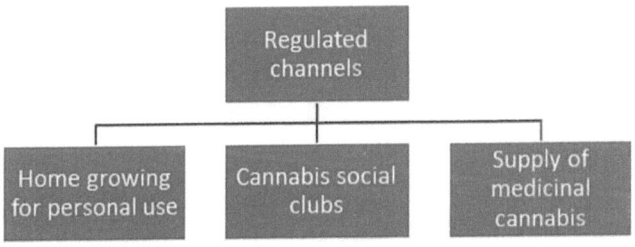

Figure 3: Three Regulated Channels for Cannabis Production and Distribution

2.1. Home Growing for Strict Personal Use

Regulating the cultivation and possession of cannabis for strict personal use is an exceptionally efficient way to reduce the dangers connected with the illegal cannabis market.

In this scenario, every *citizen of age* is allowed to cultivate a limited amount of cannabis for personal use. A citizen is a natural person who has a permanent home or address in the country and who is registered at an address in a municipality in the country.

The maximum amount of allowed plants for personal use is *limited to six plants per (adult) member* of the household, irrespective of whether the plants are cultivated inside or outside, and irrespective of the maturity of the plants (cuttings, young plants or full-grown plants).

One can also decide to have all the plants (up to a maximum of six plants) or some of them cultivated by a cannabis social club **(see Section 2.2)**. An adult is not allowed to possess more than six plants – whether they are cultivated at home or "looked after" by a cannabis social club. Residents can choose to cultivate a few plants at home (for example 4 plants) and entrust the cultivation of some plants (in the same example 2 plants) to a social club.

The grower for strict personal use is allowed to possess an unlimited amount of cannabis seeds at all times. The sale of cannabis seeds is not prohibited. The Single Convention on Narcotic Drugs of 1961 also states that cannabis seeds are beyond the reach of the ban order.

In case of home growing, the used electrical equipment (grow lights, carbon filters, automated irrigation systems, and so on) for this purpose should have a quality mark and must be connected in a correct and fireproof way. Tapping electricity for the meter is considered as theft and should be punished as such.

The grower for strict personal use can possess the proceeds

from these plants; in his home in a safe place, which is not accessible for minors.

The grower for strict personal use is responsible for the quality of the cannabis that he/she produces and consumes. Hints for safe growing of high quality cannabis can be made available by cannabis social clubs, prevention organizations and by the authorities.

If after some time, indications emerge that the proposed regulation of home growing generates undesirable side effects (such as leakage of home-grown cannabis to the black market or commercial practices), the policy can be adjusted, for example by lowering the maximum amount of plants, by fixing a maximum amount of cannabis that a grower for strict personal use is allowed to have at home, or by limiting the amount of grams that a user is allowed to transport or possess in public space.

Selling cultivated cannabis for personal use to a third party is considered as a commercial activity and is illegal. If an individual is caught, he/she ought to be punished with penalties that are comparable with those for illegal drug trafficking. Selling cannabis to minors is an aggravated circumstance.

A number of major limitations and rules are enforced upon the use of cannabis and specific sanctions are imposed on breaking them:

- Cannabis use or possession are only allowed for *adults*;
- *Cannabis use is not allowed in public spaces, on the shop floor and in the catering industry*, analogous to the smoking ban in many countries;
- *Youth work centers and youth centers* are public spaces: a smoking ban is applied (for tobacco and for cannabis);
- Analogous to the local and temporary application of an alcohol ban, local authorities, as part of their local case load policy, can maintain a *temporary "blowing ban"* at or around certain places, or at particular events;

- Cannabis can only be sold by *licensed distributors* (in this case the cannabis social clubs, **see Section 2.2**), and only to *residents* (in order to prevent cannabis tourism).

Other rules should be applied for people who use cannabis for medicinal purposes. This will be discussed **in Section 2.3**.

It is important to note that home growing for strict personal use is hard to regulate and its regulation is difficult to enforce. But experience has taught us that home growing creates few significant challenges. Home growing ("home grown") is particularly popular under a ban regime (as we know it nowadays) or in a legally regulated regime in which, apart from the cultivation for personal use, there are hardly any or no other legally-regulated channels. Whether the majority of cannabis users will prefer the convenience of legally-available cannabis through cannabis social clubs (see paragraph "Cannabis social clubs") or growing the plants themselves, depends on various factors. One important condition is a correct price-fixing of cannabis which is sold through the cannabis social clubs: The higher the prices of cannabis products in the clubs, the more home growing for personal use is stimulated. A second factor is the registration duty in cannabis social clubs. Experiences with the introduction of the so-called "weed pass" in the Netherlands (by which cannabis consumers were obliged to register at a *coffeeshop*) and with the regulated cannabis social clubs in Uruguay reveal that many cannabis users – after several decades of repressive policy – are suspicious with regard to registration requirements.

2.2. Cannabis Social Clubs

Cannabis consumers who don't want to or can't grow for personal use at home, can give the responsibility for taking care of their plant(s) to so-called *cannabis social clubs*. These clubs produce cannabis for their members' personal consumption.

An inhabitant can decide to have grown some or all plants (maximum six) by a cannabis social club (**see Section 2.1**).

An important challenge is to create safe and controlled environments where people can buy or consume cannabis. The availability of cannabis has to be such that the demand for cannabis can be sufficiently met, and that the illegal channels can be reduced. At the same time, the availability cannot be too high, given that this could lead to an increase in use. Distribution points should not encourage the consumption of cannabis.

2.2.1. Legally Required Organization Structure

Cannabis social clubs are nonprofit organizations that must be established and registered as such. The foundation and statutes of every cannabis social club must be published in official statute books or journals. The statutes of a cannabis association can mention that the societal goal of the association is to produce cannabis for their registered members, but of course they cannot include objectives that are contrary with public order or accepted principles of morality.

Cannabis social clubs have to meet all legal requirements for nonprofit organizations: the formulation of detailed statutes with the mandatory statutory elements, the mandatory bodies that must be established (the board and the general meeting), the members' register, the mentioning of "nonprofit organization" on all documents, the fiscal obligations (including showing the annual accounts) and so on.

In general, those who want to start a nonprofit organization have to keep in mind that the organization must have a charitable, idealistic and/or selfless objective and that the "commercial deeds" should always be of secondary importance to realizing the main objective.

In some countries, the legislator makes a distinction between different sizes of nonprofit organizations, and applies different obligations in terms of accountancy. In Belgium for example, the legislator distinguished between small, medium and large nonprofit organizations. In my model, cannabis social clubs should only be allowed as *small nonprofit organizations*. If we would apply the Belgian definition here, that means that they are not allowed to exceed one of the following three criteria:

1. an average of five full-time employers over the year;
2. receipts of 312,500 euros on an annual basis, exclusive of VAT and extraordinary revenues;
3. a balance sheet total of 1,249,500 euros.

A cannabis club has to be *established by at least three persons*: a chairperson, a secretary and a treasurer (the board). The founders must be national residents and have to be at least twenty-one years old (this means: a permanent home or address in the country and registered at an address in a municipality in the country). They cannot have any previous convictions for membership of a criminal organization, money laundering operations, blackmail or corruption, nor for serious violent crimes and drug production or distribution on a large scale. As the specific purpose is to transform the existing black market into a legally-regulated cannabis market, a previous conviction for growing cannabis is not a sufficient reason for exclusion.

To ensure the "not-for-profit" character of the cannabis clubs, we should also carefully think about defining other restrictions on board membership and governance: for example, banning people involved in the cannabis industry (or the pharmaceutical, alcohol or tobacco industries) from serving as a trustee or officer of one of these cannabis social clubs.

Before a cannabis social club can start producing and distributing cannabis products, it has to receive a *license* from the competent public body that exercises control of the cannabis market and the various actors (**see Chapter 5**). This government service visits the location and checks if the club meets all conditions and requirements (or can meet them). The government should also clearly indicate which *sanctions* are connected with breaking the different regulations and rules.

A license as a cannabis social club provides judicial guarantees and legal obligations concerning:

- the production (the cultivation);
- the safety and quality of the cannabis products;
- the transport (from the growing locations to the storage space and from the storage space to the distribution location);
- the storage;
- the distribution (sale) of cannabis to registered members.

Cannabis social clubs can take on two forms: *with and without consumption facilities*. Cannabis social clubs *with* consumption facilities have a space where the members can consume cannabis; this is not possible in cannabis clubs without consumption facilities. The rules for both forms of cannabis social clubs only differ with regard to the consumption facilities (cannabis consumption in the club) and the additional requirements for the personnel that works there.

With an eye toward obtaining a license, cannabis social clubs must submit a *complete file* with information regarding:

- all staff members of the club and their tasks and responsibilities;
- all "plant caretakers" of the club;
- The exact locations where cannabis is cultivated;
- The exact locations where cannabis is stored;

- The exact location where cannabis is distributed amongst the members and where cannabis might be used;
- The means by which cannabis is transported from the production location(s) to the distribution location, and by whom;
- The growing procedures followed by the club and the guarantees provided for safe and high quality cannabis products.

Limiting the number of cannabis social clubs in a city, municipality or region (in other words: controlling the *density of the number of clubs* in a geographical area) can have counterproductive effects. The experience with Dutch *coffeeshops* taught us that when there is limited or no supply, users will make use of illegal channels. If a government wants to limit the number of distribution points (cannabis social clubs or other), then it should take this mechanism into account.

Cannabis social clubs can play a major role in the education of users concerning the risks of different products, harm reduction, responsible use and transferal to specialized drug treatment. Staff members have extra responsibilities in cannabis social clubs where cannabis is consumed. They must meet additional *obligations with regard to training* in order to deal with people who need help and to monitor the (possibly problematic) consumption behavior of the members. Staff members who distribute cannabis, should have – by means of such training – an appropriate attitude concerning cannabis consumption, on the basis of a sound knowledge about the physical and psychosocial effects of the product. They should master the techniques needed to check the identity of people, to recognize signs of excessive consumption, and to be able to refuse supply of cannabis if necessary. They also have to know the possible sanctions when violating the law.

The experience with the alcohol and tobacco sector taught

us that pure self-regulation concerning responsible service is not enough. Cannabis sellers should strictly apply the rules in the first place and they should be a source of correct, trustworthy information and advice with regard to all sorts of issues, such as safe methods of use, the risks of driving under the influence of cannabis and so on. People should be able to find help or advice if they are worried about their cannabis use. In my view, the same principles must also be applied more consistently and strictly to alcohol and tobacco sellers.

2.2.2. Nonprofit

Cannabis social clubs are nonprofit organizations. In order to prevent these organizations from evolving into commercial organizations over the course of time, a number of specific restrictions are enforced:

- A club can have a maximum of 250 members at any time. They can use waiting lists;
- Every form of advertising for the organization, promotion of cannabis use or aggressive recruitment of members is not allowed (see Section 2.2.3);
- A club can *"take care of"* a maximum number of 1500 plants (250 members x maximum six plants) at any one time.

The restriction with regard to the maximum number of members comes from the experience with some cannabis social clubs in Spain. Such clubs have been operating in a grey legal zone and are not regulated to this day. This led to the creation of cannabis clubs with thousands of members with merely commercial purposes. Limiting the number of members can prevent cannabis clubs from changing into purely commercial organizations.

Jonathan Caulkins, a drug policy expert at Carnegie Mellon

University in Pittsburgh, argued that "what society should want is to undercut the black market without promoting greater problem use. For-profit companies do the former, but not the latter. Not-for-profits are more likely to respect these twin aims, particularly if the law requires them to write that dual mission explicitly into their charter before obtaining a license to operate in the cannabis market".

Another colleague and friend of mine, dr. Chris Wilkins from Massey University (New Zealand), recently proposed a "not-for-profit" regulatory model for legal recreational cannabis based on the regulation of gaming machine gambling in his own country. He carefully thought about how excess revenue by the licensed "not-for-profit" cannabis societies in his model should be redistributed to serve the public good. In his model, cannabis societies should be required to distribute a minimum 20% of the gross revenue from cannabis sales to publicly available local drug treatment services, with a further 20% given to authorized community purposes including drug prevention, community health services and sports and cultural groups. Cannabis societies would also be required to transfer 5% of gross cannabis sales to cannabis research and evaluation. A further 5% of gross cannabis sales would be allocated to the cannabis regulatory agency to support auditing and enforcement activity. Underfunding of the regulator can be a weakness of the model, as it can result in limited enforcement activity. It is important that the regulator be sufficient resourced to fully investigate and prosecute fraudulent behavior. Under the regime proposed by Chris Wilkins, the government would receive 20% of the money from gross cannabis sales for licensing and levies to support the funding of public services to address the wider health and social impacts of cannabis use, such as additional health and social services. The cannabis societies would retain approximately 30% of gross sales revenues to cover their operating costs.

To ensure that the money from cannabis sales goes back to

local communities, Wilkins proposes that eighty percent of the community grants from cannabis sales would be required to be spent in the region where they are collected.

2.2.3. No Promotion

In the last few years, it has been scientifically proven that alcohol marketing – both the traditional forms of direct marketing in print and TV media, and indirect marketing through internet, new social media and mobile telephony – has an impact on drinking. Advertising increases the chances that a proportion of young people will start to drink, or there is a chance – if they are already drinking – that they will drink more. Alcohol advertising not only influences the individual's consumption but also the social norms around alcohol. This in turn influences again the attitude towards alcohol. The more young people think that drinking alcohol is widely accepted, the greater the chance that they will start to drink and continue to drink more and more. The same goes for cannabis and other substances; and that is why we must enforce restrictions concerning advertising or promotion.

A large variety of volume and content restrictions to regulated alcohol marketing exists throughout the world. These regulations can be embedded by law (legislation or statutory regulations), by voluntary codes (self-regulation or non-statutory regulations), or by a combination of the two (co-regulation). Although these existing regulations show a large variety of both content and volume restrictions, many elements can broadly speaking be applied to the cannabis social clubs in this scenario as well.

Cannabis social clubs are consequently *not allowed to advertise their products through direct or indirect channels or to promote cannabis use.* This means that they cannot develop or sell merchandising, that they can't apply direct marketing strategies by mail or apps, and that the information on their website:

- Must not link up connections between cannabis use and an improvement of physical performances or motorized driving;
- Must not give the impression that cannabis use contributes to social or sexual success;
- Should not encourage excessive cannabis use nor put abstinence or moderate cannabis use in a bad light;
- Must not emphasize the high THC-percentage of cannabis products as a good quality;
- Must not represent cannabis products as a means for conquering dangerous situations;
- Should not suggest that cannabis products are a necessary condition to make daily life more happy nor to create a festive atmosphere;
- Has to provide an educational, harm reductive message ("Use your head while using cannabis");
- Should not focus on minors and especially must not show any minors using cannabis;
- Should not use any drawings or marketing techniques that refer to personalities that are particularly popular or are quite the thing with minors, nor drawings or marketing techniques in which images or statements are included that belong to the mainstream culture of minors.

Cannabis social clubs are not allowed to advertise for cannabis products (or other narcotics, such as tobacco or alcohol) in their rooms.

2.2.4. Membership Criteria

Residents must be *at least eighteen years* old to become a member of a cannabis social club. Members have to be *national residents* in order to prevent a pull factor for cannabis entrepreneurs and consumers and export to foreign countries (cannabis tourism from the neighboring countries). They must have a permanent home or address in the country and have to be registered in a municipality. Citizens can only be a member of one club in order to prevent the cannabis shopping of people between different clubs. On the basis of the member registers (**see Section 2.2.13**), the supervisory government can verify if people try to join several clubs.

If someone registers at a cannabis social club, he/she has to fill in a registration form, in which he/she states:

- That he/she is *informed about the risks and negative effects of cannabis on health.* The cannabis social clubs are responsible for a complete and a correct supply of information concerning this; it is advisable that they join a formal collaboration with an authorized organization that is specialized in drug prevention or treatment.
- That he/she has *knowledge about of the current national drug legislation.* This includes that he/she knows that distributing cannabis outside the legally regulated channels is punishable, as well as passing on or reselling cannabis that he/she acquires at the club, to others (including minors). The cannabis social clubs are responsible for a complete and a correct supply of information concerning this; they can formally collaborate with local police forces.
- That he/she *voluntarily* joins a cannabis social club.
- That he/she *knows about the house rules of the cannabis social club* and the possible sanctions when breaking them.
- That he/she agrees with *the registration of a number of basic sociodemographic and identity data.* The cannabis clubs should protect and keep these data in conformity with the prevailing privacy legislation and must be able to supply it if required by the police or inspection services. They cannot and should not share or pass on these data to a third party

(such as employers, insurance companies, national health services and so on).

- That he/she agrees with an *intake interview with regard to his/her personal cannabis consumption pattern* before registration at the club, and with a *continuous registration* of the amount of cannabis that he/she obtains through the cannabis club. The cannabis clubs have to protect and keep these data in conformity with the privacy legislation and must be able to supply it if required by the police or inspection services. They cannot share or pass on these data to a third party. The cannabis social clubs can, on the basis of these data and with an assumption of "problematic use", voluntarily give advice to their members or refer the people concerned to the specialized organizations for drug prevention or treatment. These data can also – but only anonymously – be used for scientific research, for example as part of evaluation studies of the regulated cannabis model (**see Chapter 4**).

2.2.5. Production of Cannabis by Clubs

Cannabis social clubs or people who work for them are not actually the "owners" of the plants they cultivate; *they "take care" of the plants of their members*. These members remain the owners of their personal plants at any time. The club employs "plant caretakers" (growers) who cultivate and take care of the plants on behalf of the members (**see Section 2.2.7**).

A cannabis social club is never allowed to take care of more than six plants per registered member. It must always be clear which members possess which plants during the whole production and distribution process. This has to be done by means of a watertight registration system and a unique identification system (a unique barcode per member attached to the plants and the final cannabis products) throughout the whole process (from seed to harvested cannabis).

The cannabis plants should be cultivated according to growing procedures that offer the most guarantees for public health. Concretely, this means that cultivation must be undertaken according to the *rules and regulations of organic farming*, and thus only biological additives (such as nutrients or pesticides) can be used. The strict regulations with regard to the use of herbicides or Plant Growth Regulators (PGRs), the use of fertilizers and of genetically-modified organisms that are enforced upon organic farming, must be applied here. The government can enforce additional regulations on the basis of advancing scientific understandings.

The cannabis social club should establish the growing procedures followed in a protocol that has to be respected by all "plant caretakers", under penalty of exclusion of the club. The club itself is responsible for regular inspections of the growing locations and for checking the procedures followed by the plant caretakers. Agencies responsible for the safety of food products regularly inspect food producers and catering businesses. This is also the case for the supervisory authority that will have to supervise periodically in order to check if, and to what extent, the cannabis clubs stick to the regulations.

2.2.6. Technical Design of the Growing Location

The plants should be cultivated in a *non-publicly accessible, closed and discretely-designed location*. The specific number of plants per growing location has to be decided in consultation with the cannabis club. The club must take appropriate measures to sufficiently protect the growing location(s) against theft. Every plant should have a proof of ownership of a registered club member.

A growing location is allowed to have a maximum of 1.500 plants.

The growing location can only be accessed by the plant caretaker(s) and the employers of the cannabis social club. The location has to be *fireproof* (electrical ballasts, fire extinguisher or blanket, smoke detector if necessary), odorless (carbon filter, hermetical space) and it should not cause *any noise or smell nuisance* (suction in a "soft box" or silencer) or other inconveniences for the neighbors.

Power supply must be installed in a correct and legal way. The license will be suspended immediately in case of violations (theft of electricity).

2.2.7. Demands on Plant "Caretakers"

The plant caretakers must be national residents of *at least twenty-one years old* (with a permanent address or residence in the country and must be registered in a municipality). They *cannot have any previous convictions* for membership of a criminal organization, money laundering operations, blackmail or corruption, nor for serious violent crimes and drug production or distribution on a large scale. As the specific purpose is to transform the existing black market into a legally regulated cannabis market, a previous conviction for growing cannabis is not a sufficient reason for exclusion.

Plant caretakers must be a registered member of the club and consequently cannot be a member of more than one club. Plant caretakers cannot be employed by more than one club.

Plant caretakers have – like every adult resident in the country – the right to cultivate a maximum of six plants for personal use in their own house. They must be able to indicate which plants are for personal use and which plants are on behalf of the cannabis social club.

The cannabis social club concludes a contract with the plant caretakers in which the concrete rights and duties of both parties are stated, including with regard to:

- the enforced minimum requirements of the government concerning growing procedures and design of the growing location;
- the enforced additional requirements of the club concerning growing procedures and design of the growing location;
- the exclusive character of the relation between the plant caretaker and the club (a plant caretaker is allowed to only work for one club);
- following the agreed production volumes (the maximum number of plants per cultivation, among other things);
- the liability of both parties towards the members of the club in case of crop failure, theft or damage to plants;
- the obligations concerning quality control of the produced cannabis;
- the liability of both parties towards any interested party (the government, the members of the club) in case of not respecting the minimum quality norms of the cannabis products;
- the agreements concerning reimbursement of the expenses of the plant caretaker (for example rent for the growing location, purchase of cultivation equipment and so on), as well as the honorarium of the plant caretaker;
- the required registration and administration for the plant caretaker.

2.2.8. Cannabis Products and Preparations

Cannabis exists in different kinds of preparations:

- *Marijuana* consists of dried, crushed leaves and buds. It looks like fine to coarse tea and is grey-green to green-brown in color. There are a lot of cannabis varieties available, differing a lot in quality and in THC and CBD content (from less strong to very strong cannabis varieties). Marijuana can be smoked (whether with tobacco or not), vaporized, eaten (mostly processed in food or drinks) or processed into a whole range of other products (see below). THC is the abbreviation of *tetrahydrocannabinol*, the pharmacologically active substance. CBD is the abbreviation of *cannabidiol*.
- *Hash (or hashish)* is created by pressing the resin of the buds together in a small block. These blocks are colored from light brown to black. Hash usually contains more THC than marijuana, but the purity and the resin potency differ. Hash can be smoked in a pipe, smoked with tobacco or other herb products in a joint (a hand-rolled cannabis cigarette), vaporized, eaten or processed in food.
- *Hash oil* feels a bit sticky and is acquired through alcoholic distillation of cannabis. In addition to this, there are *other concentrates* – definitely the ones that are obtained by the most recent hi-tech extraction methods – that can be very strong. Some even contain more than 80% THC. For example butane hash oil (BHO), which is made with the extraction substance butane, is a very strong cannabis concentrate that is sometimes used in a process that is called "dabbing": at which the user drips the concentrate on a hot surface and inhales the vapors.
- *Cannabis edibles*: Marijuana is edible in its raw form, but it happens more often that the active ingredients are dissolved in oil or butter and used in countless prepared food products (cakes, brownies, cookies, lollipops and so on). A lot of drinks are also infused with cannabis oil or tinctures.

- *Other cannabis preparations*: In recent years, a lot of new preparations were developed for the purpose of medicinal cannabis use: sprays, tinctures, sublingual tablets or strips, all sorts of tea, tonic drinks and soft drinks that often contain cannabis tinctures of variable strength. In Colorado, shrewd businessmen have made use of the minimally regulated cannabis market in order to develop cannabis sweets, lollipops, shampoos and so on.

The risks of cannabis use are both connected with the nature of the cannabis preparations (and the potency of these products) and the method of use. Cannabis products can be used in different ways:

- The most common means of consumption is smoking cannabis, either in a sort of pipe, in a joint that only contains cannabis, or in which marijuana or hash is mixed with tobacco. Smoking cannabis is a popular method of use, because it's easy and not expensive. The effect of the product is quickly felt and allows the user to easily control the dose. Preparing and sharing a joint is also a social, shared experience to many. Burning cannabis (and everything with which it is mixed) results of course in the creation of all sorts of combustion products, such as tar (with carcinogenic benzene among other things) and carbon monoxide. Inhaling the smoke increases the health risks for the throat and lungs. Furthermore, smoking joints in which tobacco and cannabis are mixed increases the risks of long-term nicotine addiction.
- The active ingredients of cannabis can also be released and inhaled in the form of a *water vapor*, so that the most toxic components of the smoke are avoided when burning cannabis in pipes or joints. This happens because of the use of a vaporizer: A device that heats cannabis to a temperature

that is high enough to set free the volatile cannabinoids as a vapor, but not high enough to have the cannabis burned. Research into vaporizers and e-cigarettes demonstrates that vaporizing cannabis or nicotine decreases the respiratory symptoms and the risks of smoking. Nevertheless, research is necessary concerning these devices and the long-term consequences of this method of use. The devices, for that matter, are not sufficiently standardized and approved.

- Cannabis is also *edible* (in all sorts of food preparations), by which the active ingredients are absorbed through the stomach and the digestive system. In contrast with smoking or inhaling the vapor, the effects of cannabis occur later (from twenty minutes to one hour, dependent on the kind of food and if you had eaten before that). Eating cannabis is much safer with regard to the damaging consequences for the throat and lungs (since there are none), but then again the consumer has much less control over the dose he/she takes. If consequently a cannabis consumer does not wait long enough to see which effect the cannabis produces, he/she runs the risk of consuming too much cannabis too fast (with possible negative or unpleasant consequences).

We have to keep in mind some important conclusions with regard to the nature of the connection between the risks and the kind of cannabis products and/or the method of use of cannabis:

- There is a clear relation between the dose and the risks of cannabis: the more a person uses, the greater the risks;
- The risks are influenced by the *knowledge of the user* (about the different cannabis products, the different methods of use and the risks) and the extent to which the user can control the dose;

- The *quickness* by which the effects are produced, varies with the method of use and the impact on the nature of the experience and the extent to which the user can control the dose;
- *The health consequences for the lungs* that are linked with smoking cannabis are comparable with those of smoking tobacco. After all, smoking is a burning process (called pyrolysis) and whatever an individual smokes, this is always unhealthy, so detrimental substances are formed that are left behind as a form of tar in his/her lungs. When cannabis is not mixed with tobacco, one could substantiate that the dependency towards the product decreases. After all, both THC (the active element of cannabis) and nicotine (the active element of tobacco) increase the chances of dependence, especially psychological. On the other hand, we have to emphasize that the health consequences for the lungs are significantly reduced when inhaling vaporized cannabis instead of cannabis smoke. This is also the case with the consumption of edible cannabis preparations. Smoking is unhealthy, without any exception, because there is a causal connection with lung cancer (among other things) due to the tar formed during the burning process.

A regulated market has to keep in mind the above-mentioned points, and a diversified regulation of different kinds of cannabis products (and the way they are used) must serve to influence consumer patterns in the best possible way, so that the safest products and the safest methods are used.

As I advocate a strictly-regulated cannabis market, I propose the following principles:

- Cannabis social clubs can only produce *a limited range of marijuana and hash products* (of low, medium and high potency) and distribute these amongst their members. They are not allowed to offer or sell any other concentrated preparations such as cannabis oil, tinctures or food infused with cannabis. Users that want edible cannabis products can easily produce these products at home, for that matter;

- Cannabis social clubs are not allowed to offer pre-rolled joints (in which cannabis and tobacco is mixed);
- Cannabis products must meet the requirements that are dictated to organically grown agricultural products; they should not contain any chemical-synthetic aromatic substances, colorings and flavorings or preservatives;
- Cannabis social clubs are responsible for *promoting the least harmful methods of use*, by only allowing the use of vaporizers in the rooms of the club (and not smoking cannabis in "joints" or pipes) among other things;
- The clubs are also responsible for supplying adequate product information and promoting harm reductive strategies in the club (through the mandatory instruction leaflet with the cannabis they distribute);
- As soon as vaporizer devices will be controlled and approved by the government (for example with a quality label), clubs could also offer these delivery tools.

2.2.9. Requirements with regard to Quality and Potency of the Cannabis Products

In a regulated cannabis market, the potency of the cannabis products has to be controlled and should be monitored in a reliable and consistent way. It should be ensured that consumers are informed accurately about the potency of the products they consume, about the potential effects and risks and about the ways in which they can reduce the risks. Finally, minimizing the potential risks of extraordinary strong cannabis products should be an important objective.

Setting up a maximum limit concerning THC in cannabis products is, because of various reasons, not obvious and exceptionally hard to enforce, but nevertheless I suggest some limits are imposed (**see figure 4**).

	Maximum THC level*	Maximum CBD level
Marijuana	15%	1%
Hash	30%	5%

* Including the precursor of THC, known as THCQ (this is tetrahydrocannabinolic acid and is converted to THC by smoking or drying the plant)

Figure 4: Hypothetical Maximum THC and CBD Levels in Marijuana and Hash

There must be *regular tests of cannabis products* that are distributed by the cannabis social clubs; this should happen by taking unannounced, randomized samples by an independent organ or laboratory appointed by the government. The intensity of the necessary quality tests will depend, after a while, on the extent to which the clubs have stuck to the required limits, but the control should be intensive when implementing the regulated system.

The production and especially the distribution of cannabis products that significantly differ from the potency that is indicated on the packing or the instruction leaflet, must be considered as serious violations of the license. The government should indicate clearly which margins of error are tolerable and what the penalties for violations will be (for example which violations will lead to a withdrawal of the license for the club).

All cannabis products have to be clearly provided with information about their potency, such as the THC and CBD levels. This information must be backed up with information about the possible risks. I propose a simple numerical scale (from category 1 to 3), that indicates the different potencies (and THC/CBD levels) (**see figure 5**).

Potency label	THC levels	Maximum CBD levels
1	0-5%	1%
2	6-10%	1%
3	11-15%	1%

Figure 5: Hypothetical Numerical Scale with regard to Potency
of Cannabis Products (THC/CBD Levels)

2.2.10. Requirements Concerning Packing

Although the risk of accidental consumption of cannabis products by children is relatively small (and de facto rarely occurs), the cannabis social clubs have to meet certain requirements concerning the packing of cannabis (that they distribute to their members). These requirements should be defined by the competent authorities for public health, but meanwhile I formulate some proposals:

1. All cannabis products must be sold in *non-transparent, resealable and childproof plastic containers*, comparable with packages that are used for some medicines, household products or food. The packing has to be such that rogue persons or ignorant children can't tamper with it (*"tamper proof"*).

2. The *information on the packing* must be based on the existing norms for medicines and on the lessons from the experiences with packing tobacco products. This means that the packing:

- has to provide a clear warning concerning the *health risks of the product*;
- *must not include a branding or design*, in other words: no brand-specific logos, colors or fonts ("plain packaging"), because these could encourage use or could increase the temptation;
- Should provide *a clear description of the cannabis preparation* (marijuana or hash);
- must provide clear information about the *potency of the product*: the THC and CBD level (in terms of percentages);
- Has to provide clear information about the *storage life of the product*.

3. All cannabis products that are distributed through the cannabis social club should be accompanied by an *instruction leaflet* that contains the following information:

- major *effects and side effects* (the positive and negative effects; the effects of different doses; possible differences in effects by different users, depending on the age, experience with the product, body weight, and so on);
- *general risks* (concerning dependency, breathing, mental health; risks for people with predetermined medical disorders);
- *secondary risks* (such as reduced competence for driving a car, operating machines or carrying out other professional tasks; risks for pregnant women and their unborn child; risks with regard to accidental consumption by children);
- *Harm reduction: How the risks should be minimized* (a description of safer methods of use and of safer products and

preparations, how to moderate use, and the risks of poly drug use);

- *Contraindications* (the risks of cannabis use with alcohol, with tobacco, with medicines whether or not prescribed and with illegal substances);
- Where to find *help or advice* (contact information and website addresses of relevant treatment and prevention organizations).

Rules concerning packing and instruction leaflets have to be legally established and must be actively enforced through controls of the supervisory body (**see Chapter 5**). Cannabis social clubs that do not stick to the regulations may lose their license or can be prosecuted, comparable with the way that tobacco producers and pharmaceutical companies can be sanctioned.

2.2.11. Storage and Transport of Cannabis

Cannabis social clubs can temporarily store cannabis products (for example between the harvest and the moment of distribution amongst the members). Obviously, a club is not allowed to store more cannabis than is legally allowed according to the norms concerning the maximum number of members (250 members) and plants (maximum six plants per member). If cannabis amounts are stored, this must be done in a location confirmed by the government that is not accessible for minors or third parties and sufficiently secured against theft. During the storage of cannabis, the club must also be able to indicate who the owners (the members) of the cannabis are, and which amount belongs to which registered member.

Clubs can only transport their products between predetermined growing locations, storage locations and the location where cannabis is distributed amongst the members. A club is not allowed to transport more cannabis than is legally allowed according to the norms concerning the maximum number of members and plants. Cannabis products must be transported in a neutral car (without promotion), in a safe way and sufficiently secured against theft. During the transport of cannabis, the club always must be able to present the necessary documents confirming the fact it is a legally-licensed cannabis club. It should also be able to indicate who the plant owners (the members) are and which amount belongs to which registered member.

2.2.12. Distribution

Clubs can only distribute self-produced products, given that they work on the basis of the principle that the members have entrusted the maintenance of their plant(s) to the cannabis clubs. In the first instance (the first phase), these organizations are not allowed to import cannabis products from other countries or purchase them through other (illegal) channels.

The distribution of cannabis products by cannabis social clubs can happen in two ways: (1) by means of *"exchange marts" at regular times*; (2) by continuous *sale during opening hours*.

Cannabis social clubs that apply the principle of the exchange marts organize events on a regular basis when the members can collect their own cannabis. Cannabis social clubs can also apply a system of opening hours, by which the members can pick up small amounts of cannabis.

There is very consistent evidence concerning alcohol regulation that limiting the number of opening days and hours is an effective means to reduce alcohol-related damage. Consequently, I believe we need to enforce some restrictions upon cannabis social clubs, but in a balanced way, in order that there is a sufficient supply of cannabis (and people don't have to supply again by way of the black market).

Anyhow, the clubs and the members are restricted to a *maximum amount of cannabis per month*. This amount must be high enough in order to prevent members from making extra purchases on the black market. At the same time, the maximum allowed amount of cannabis per person should not be too high, so that they won't resell it to a third party. I propose a limit of 60 grams of cannabis per person per month. The clubs are responsible for a correct registration of the quantities that is collected by every member every month.

Clubs that distribute more cannabis to their members than is legally allowed, risk the loss of their license and in serious cases prosecution for illegal trade in cannabis. Members of clubs that are caught reselling cannabis to a third party (especially minors), also risk being prosecuted for illegal drug dealing.

Cannabis social clubs that allow consumption of cannabis in the club have to fulfil some additional conditions:

- Given their extra responsibilities with regard to recognizing signs of excessive consumption, and with regard to refusing cannabis to some members if necessary, the staff members have to meet extra *requirements concerning training*;
- The consumption rooms must display *correct and clear information* with reference to safer methods of use, the risks of cannabis use (in traffic amongst other things) and the organizations and centers where users can get help or advice;
- *No other drugs* can be sold in the consumption rooms: no tobacco, no alcohol (and of course no other illegal drugs);
- No display of promotion or advertising for cannabis products is allowed in the consumption room (**see Section 2.2.3**).
- The boarding on the street side or the signposting to the consumption room should only be functional and not aimed on advertising or tempting passers-by. In Washington, the

signposting must not include references to cannabis (such as the well-known green cannabis leaf), but only the firm or club name.

2.2.13. Transparent Administration and Accounting

Transparency is necessary for showing both the members and the supervisory bodies how, why, by whom, for what and by which motives, decisions are taken by the administration. For that purpose, every organization must keep the following documents and be able to hand them over to the controlling public servants of the supervisory body (**See also Chapter 5**);

- An *up-to-date member register*: the membership of a cannabis club should go hand in hand with the registration of personal information. The club is responsible for the protection of this information according to the legal norms. The supervisory bodies are allowed to check and look into this information;
- The *identification documents and the licenses* for the plant caretakers and other active workers;
- A *sale and distribution register*: an anonymous register in which the produced and distributed quantities are kept up to date;
- A *transparent and correct accounting*: the organization is responsible for a meticulous administration and a detailed accounting that can be checked by the members, by tax authorities and by the supervisory body;
- Reports of *all member meetings*.

2.3. Supply of Cannabis for Medicinal Purposes

For many centuries, the cannabis plant has been used in a medicinal context for its sedative, sleep-inducing, antidepressant, pain killing, anticonvulsive, antiemetic, anti-inflammatory, antispasmodic and appetite stimulating qualities. Scientific literature offers a lot of evidence that cannabis with a high CBD level is effective against pain and spasms, for example in the case of patients with multiple sclerosis (MS), and it also seems to be effective against inflammation. Cannabis with a high level of THC is especially effective for disorders, such as Gilles de la Tourette syndrome, therapy resistant glaucoma and for complaints with regard to weight loss, sickness and vomiting. For that reason, some cancer patients also use cannabis to reduce symptoms or side effects of their treatment.

2.3.1. Extension of the Legal Availability of Medicinal Cannabis Products

In some countries, including my own (Belgium), medicinal cannabis products are only available under very strict conditions (**see Chapter 1**), and in other countries medicinal cannabis is completely outlawed. This means medicinal cannabis is not legally available for several groups of patients, who consequently turn to the illegal market to supply themselves with cannabis. *A broader, legally-regulated availability of cannabis for medicinal use for specific groups of patients is desirable.*

2.3.2. Home Growing for Personal Use for Medical Purposes

If we presume that home growing for strict personal (recreational) use is regulated, then this also means that patients themselves can cultivate just as many plants for medicinal purposes. It is advisable to point out to the patients as much as possible the risks of consuming cannabis that is not cultivated according to pharmaceutical requirements, as its quality and safety are not guaranteed.

As patients that use cannabis for medicinal purposes often need larger quantities, *an increase of the maximum amount of allowed plants for these cases* can be taken into consideration. The patient has to request a special exemption or license for that, in which the serious medical disorder or condition is verified with official certificates and in which there must be proof that the attending physician is consulted and agrees with the consumption of cannabis for medical purposes.

Finally, I want to point out that home growing and harvesting of cannabis and preparing cannabis products is just not possible for some patients because of their state of health and syndrome. The American *principle of "caregivers"* can be applied in such exceptional cases. This principle allows a housemate (a partner, a family member) to grow cannabis on behalf of the patient. This person must obtain a special license or exemption.

2.3.4. Strict Division Between Recreational and Medicinal Cannabis Channels

At the same time, I want to emphasize the importance of a strict separation between the production and distribution of cannabis *for medical use,* and the production and distribution of cannabis *for recreational use.* We should avoid a situation in which cannabis for medical purposes leads to illegal markets or to legal markets for recreational use. Furthermore, it may never be the intention that under the guise of supplying medicinal cannabis, a parallel market for recreational cannabis is actually being created, which has been the case in some American states. For this reason I also argue for a well-defined qualitative and quantitative composition for medicinal cannabis.

2.3.5. Cannabis Products of Pharmaceutical Quality

Obviously, when cannabis as a medicine or a medical treatment of symptoms is consumed, the *product must be of pharmaceutical quality*. I propose that this form of cannabis has a THC:CBD ratio of 1:1 and that level of both THC and CBD is 5%. A state can decide to be inspired by the Dutch model with regard to medicinal cannabis, in which the *Bureau Medicinal Cannabis* is responsible as a government organization for the production of cannabis for medicinal and scientific purposes. The company Bedrocan is since 2003 the only one that has been producing medicinal cannabis for the Dutch Ministry of Public Health, Welfare and Sport.

The requirements for the preparation of medicines are legally enforced in most countries, and consequently medicinal cannabis products should also meet these requirements. No medicine can be commercialized *without registration or license*. In Belgium for example, this license is granted by the minister of Public Health, after advice from the Medicine commission within the Federal Agency for Medicines and Health Products (FAMHP), or the European Community, possibly after advice from the Committee for Medicinal Products for Human Use or the Committee for Medicinal Products for Veterinary Use (CVMP) within the European Medicines Agency (EMA). The appointed experts within these different bodies evaluate *the quality, the control and the efficiency of all medicines* on the basis of scientific data presented by the applicant. During this evaluation, they rely on the scientific norms that are operative on a European or international level. The license for distributing a medicine is granted to medicines of which the quality, the security and the efficiency are clearly demonstrated.

In Europe, arguments concerning the security and the efficiency of a medicine can be presented to the competent authority in different ways:

- By a *complete file*: the applicant presents the pharmacological, toxicological and clinical studies when applying for a license of an original medicine;
- By a *generic file*: if an active element is allowed in one member state of the European Union for at least ten years, and if in addition the patent is expired, the applicant can refer to the results of the studies carried out with the original medicine (the reference medicine), provided that both are "essentially equal;"
- By a *bibliographic file*: with reference to published scientific literature which proves that the medicine can be accepted concerning its pharmacological, toxicological and clinical aspects. This possibility can only be applied if the active element has been used as a medicine in medical practice in the European Union for at least ten years (*"well established use"*) and moreover is recognized as effective and safe.

The applicant should demonstrate for every medicine that the manufacturer is able to produce a product of *sufficient and constant quality* and there must be guarantees that this quality remains until the proposed expiry date. The following aspects of the medicine have to be discussed in the submitted file: the pharmaceutical development, the production process, the control of and the stability of the active element, the control of the production process and all ingredients (including packing) and the control and the stability of the medicine. Every modification of these elements, after the medicine has been launched, has to take place with a license.

Producers of medicines (legal drugs) are subjected to *regular inspections*. In Europe for example, they have to meet the European requirements concerning *"Good Manufacturing Practices"* (GMP) and are only allowed to produce medicines if they have a GMP-certificate. If they do not meet these requirements, then the GMP-certificate will be revoked and the producer concerned cannot produce any more medicines. The controls by the national agency (or agencies) for medicines and health products must ensure that every resident has access to high-quality, efficient and safe medicines.

2.3.6. Cannabis Only Available on Prescription

In my opinion, medicinal cannabis products have to be guided and supervised by a doctor and thus must be prescription-only products. The effects of medicinal cannabis differ from person to person. For that reason, a doctor has to determine in consultation with the patient which variety is the most suitable, how much and how many times per day he/she needs medicinal cannabis, and how the patient uses it. The doctor in attendance also has an eye for interactions of medicinal cannabis products with other medicines that a patient takes as part of his/her treatment.

2.3.7. Cannabis Supply only through Pharmacies

Medicinal cannabis supply should only happen via pharmacies. Pharmacies are not allowed to supply medicinal cannabis products without a medical prescription. The pharmacist must make sure that the patient correctly applies his/her treatment. This includes for example that he/she explains to the client when and how he/she should take his/her medicinal cannabis product, that he/she warns the client for possible side effects and that he/she has an eye for interactions with other medicines that the client takes.

2.3.8. Medicinal Cannabis Through Cannabis Social Clubs

Nowadays, there are some cannabis social clubs in Belgium that only produce and distribute cannabis for medicinal use. Other clubs mainly serve recreational users, but also have some members that use it for therapeutic reasons (**see Chapter 1**).

On the basis of the two important principles as defended above – in particular, the importance of a strict division between the cultivation and distribution of cannabis *for medical use* and the cultivation and distribution of cannabis *for recreational use* on the one hand, and the principle that medicinal applications of cannabis should happen under the supervision of a doctor in attendance on the other hand – I want to argue that *the production and distribution of cannabis for medicinal purposes by cannabis social clubs should be forbidden* and only be made possible through the channels mentioned above (production by the pharmaceutical industry, subject to the requirement of a prescription from a doctor, available through pharmacies).

The option in which there are cannabis social clubs that are only responsible for the production and distribution of medicinal cannabis, is an alternative that requires extra investigation. The cannabis products that the clubs supply to patients of course must meet all pharmaceutical requirements. Furthermore, extra conditions (such as the obligatory formal cooperation with doctors) should be enforced. The regulatory framework must be formulated in such a way that there are no cannabis social clubs that engage in the distribution of medicinal cannabis merely for the money. In my opinion, the production and distribution of cannabis for medicinal purposes through cannabis clubs that focus on recreational consumers should be forbidden, with an eye toward a strict division between medicinal and recreational cannabis.

CHAPTER 4

Evaluation and Adjustment

The scenario presented in the previous chapter can be considered a first phase in a lengthy process of reform. It is very likely that any new cannabis policy will suffer from teething problems, and lessons will be learnt from its growing pains. That is why I argue in this chapter, that the model described previously can and should be adjusted after a serious and independent evaluation of the implementation of the model and its effects on numerous parameters. In a second phase, one must verify which parts of the new regulatory regime should become less or more rigid, and if it is a wise decision to create additional channels for cannabis production and distribution, or not.

1. Independent and Scientific Evaluation

It is especially important to have the implementation of a new cannabis policy and its side effects *evaluated by independent scientists*. Such scientific evaluation of the whole process and the effects in the short, medium and long term can lead to the adjustment of the policy if desired (both concerning the creation of new restrictions and government interventions and liberalizing the current rules).

The success of the cannabis ban and the repressive approach is always measured by indicators and statistics that rather reflect processes or (police) activities, such as the number of arrests, reports or municipal administrative fines, the number of discovered plantations or the amounts of cannabis confiscated, or the penalty. Such indicators do show us how much effort the authorities have made or how forcefully they acted, but the stats do not illustrate how successful the state is in improving public health.

With an eye to a critical evaluation of the new policy, *relevant and measurable indicators* must be formulated with regard to all aspects of the cannabis market and its functioning. These indicators should refer to the objectives of a new cannabis policy as listed in the introduction.

- Does the new cannabis policy lead to the reduction of illegal channels, the weakening and in the long term the elimination of the black market in cannabis, and the deprivation of an important source of income to organized crime and their economic power?
- Does the new cannabis policy lead to better control of the composition, the purity, the potency and the quality of cannabis in general, for the protection of public health?
- Does the new model lead to an improved control of the marketing strategies of cannabis producers?
- To what extent do the legal cannabis producers and distributers stick to the legally-enforced regulations and limitations? To what extent is a relaxing or tightening of certain regulations imperative?
- What are the effects of the new cannabis policy on the prevalence of cannabis use and on the patterns of cannabis consumption (in particular amongst young people)?
- What are the economic effects concerning expenses and incomes? Does the new model lead to more cost efficiency and investments based on scientific evidence in efficient prevention, in the reduction of the demand and harm reduction, and to fewer expenses in the tracing, prosecution and punishment of illegal producers?

- What are the effects of the new policy on all sorts of nuisance and criminality?
- What are the effects of the new policy on (the overload of) the criminal justice system and the (overpopulation of) the penitentiary system?
- What are the effects with regard to the reduction of pollution as a result of large-scale illegal cannabis production (cannabis plantations)?
- What are the effects of the policy on the role and the tasks of prevention workers and social workers and on the accessibility of their target audience?

The answers to all these questions have to be used in order to evaluate the new policy and to adjust the regulatory framework in the light of new evidence.

2. Adjustment of the Model

Setting a new course does not happen overnight. It must be phased and it should be implemented cautiously, based on experiments, by which the policy is carefully adjusted and adapted according to the indications that become visible. If a policy does not work, it must be reviewed and, if necessary, it should even be revoked.

After a careful evaluation based on the parameters mentioned above (**see Section 1**), it consequently must be verified whether and to what extent:

- the rules concerning home growing (the maximum number of allowed plants) should be liberalized or tightened;
- the rules concerning the legally mandatory organization structure of cannabis social clubs have to be adjusted;
- the legally provided conditions in order to have a license as a cannabis social club must be adjusted;

- the limitations concerning size and promotion strategies for cannabis social clubs ought to be liberalized or tightened;
- the membership criteria (such as the minimum age) should be adapted;
- the production capacity and growing procedures for clubs must be revised;
- the ban on the import of cannabis products from abroad or purchase through other channels must be maintained;
- the requirements set out for the "plant caretakers" ought to be liberalized or tightened;
- the allowed range of cannabis products needs to be extended or restricted;
- requirements concerning quality and potency and concerning the packing of the cannabis products have to be adjusted;
- the rules concerning the distribution of cannabis (exchange marts, opening hours of clubs, consumption facilities within the clubs and so on) should be adjusted.

3. Creating Additional Legal Channels

It is possible that a state, on the basis of the evaluation of the effects of the new regulated model, decides to investigate the possibilities with regard to additional legal channels for cannabis production and distribution. This can be the case if it appears that the three channels that were regulated in the first phase do not suffice to meet the existing demand (and thus there remain too many opportunities and profit margins for illegal producers); or if these channels appear to be less attractive for an overly-large group of cannabis consumers in comparison with supplying themselves on the black market. After all, it is foreseeable that not all cannabis users will grow cannabis themselves, and that not all consumers will be prepared to register at a cannabis social club. This can also have to do with the observation that existing channels (such as home growing for personal use and the cannabis social clubs) insufficiently lead to a higher quality and purity of the available cannabis products, for example because the cannabis social clubs are insufficiently able to meet the quality requirements imposed by the authorities.

Additional legal channels for cannabis production and distribution can adopt different forms:

- A complete government monopoly, by which commercial players are not allowed to access the legally-regulated market;
- A commercial market with a small number (or an unlimited number) of licensed producers and similarly distributors (or outlets), in which diverse aspects may or may not be strictly regulated;
- A regulated model consisting of a mix of commercial and government monopolistic elements (in which various aspects of the market – production – commercial players are allowed and in which other aspects – sales through cannabis stores – strictly remain in the hands of the government).

CHAPTER 5

General Conditions

When a policy fails to achieve its purposes, a great deal of political, institutional, temporal, and economic capital has been wasted. This is one of the lessons we can learn from the failure of the war on drugs, and prohibitionist cannabis policies in particular. These lessons are necessary ex post observations on the war on drugs, but they must also inform any ex ante analysis of the newly proposed policy designs, instrument choices, and other policy-making variables to establish a framework for more effective cannabis policy making. Though policy success may be inhibited by a variety of procedural, programmatic, or political factors, I believe a preliminary institutional analysis of the necessary preconditions in the earlier stages of the policy cycle can help society avoid constitutionally driven policy failures and move toward institutional policy successes. Only when these institutional preconditions are achieved will the procedural, programmatic, and political components of a new cannabis policy have an opportunity to succeed. That is why I address some necessary preconditions for the implementation of the scenario presented in the previous chapters in this final chapter.

1. Supervisory Bodies

In preparation for the implementation of a new cannabis policy, the government has to set up *an independent commission of domestic and foreign experts*, in order to identify the major issues and to formulate the general recommendations with regard to the new policy. The expertise of these experts should relate to many domains: public health, drug policy, international and national law, legal cannabis production, agriculture, environmental care and monitoring and evaluation research. This panel can gradually evolve to a *task force* that supervises and formulates recommendations concerning the details and the implementation of the new cannabis policy.

As mentioned above, it is extremely important to have *evaluated* the implementation of the new cannabis policy and its side effects on a continuous basis by *independent scientists*. Sufficient resources must be provided for monitoring and evaluating the impact and must be incorporated in the regulated model from the beginning. In the face of a critical evaluation of the new policy, *relevant and measurable indicators* must be established with regard to all aspects of the cannabis market and its functioning. These should relate to the objectives of the new policy, as listed before. These monitoring data should be used to make sure that the policy and the policy modifications are screened regularly in order that there is a certain flexibility to adjust strategies in the light of new evidence.

The state must create a *supervisory body* that grants the licenses for cannabis social clubs (and in the longer term other possible license holders) and controls the compliance with all regulations. Just to clarify what I mean, let me call it the *Federal Agency for the Regulation and Control on Cannabis (FACC)*. This organization can be an equivalent or can be part of the organizations that supervise the rules concerning the production and the sale of tobacco and alcohol. Considering the large number of domains on which the regulation of cannabis can have an effect, a new umbrella organ should be created, analogous to agencies that supervise the safety of the food chain, or of medicines and health products. An *Instituto de Regulación y Control del Cannabis* (IRCA) is also established in Uruguay for that purpose.

This supervisory body should pay attention to:

- the license procedure and the license grant for cannabis social clubs;
- compliance with the regulations with regard to production, storage and distribution of cannabis products through cannabis social clubs;
- compliance with the regulations with regard to quality and safety of the legally allowed cannabis products (and its packing);
- the registration of the members (and the limitation that national (adult) residents are only allowed to join one cannabis social club);
- the price policy concerning cannabis products;
- ...

2. Clear and Proportionate Sanction System

In the scenario for a regulated cannabis market I propose here, administrative or criminal sanctions for the production, supply and possession of cannabis that take place *within* the parameters of the legal framework, are abolished. However, all activities that take place *outside* the legal framework (for example the sale of cannabis to minors and the production and distribution by non-licensed individuals or organizations) remain punishable. The government should also provide *a clear and proportionate sanction system* for producers, distributors or users that do not adhere to the rules: in particular the regulations concerning the maximum allowed amounts and allowed cannabis products, the requirements concerning quality and potency of cannabis, the regulations with regard to the packing and the instruction leaflet, the ban on advertising, marketing and branding and so on. The imposed sanctions can differ according to the severity of the violation: administrative fines, revoking of the license, or criminal sanctions.

3. Convergence of the Alcohol, Tobacco and Cannabis Policy

In recent years, various reforms were introduced regarding the regulation of alcohol and tobacco in many countries. These were usually aimed at minimizing the less regulated and purely commercial market with more restrictions (**see figure 2 in Chapter 1**). Therefore, the regulatory models for both drugs moved to the middle between the two extreme options, with on the one hand a total ban (with a complete black market) and on the other hand a free, unregulated and purely commercial market. The scenario for the regulation of cannabis I propose here also aims for a legally strictly regulated market model. It is important *to apply the same principles, based on scientific evidence about public health and harm reduction, to all drugs and to develop for every drug the most suitable regulation model.* Nowadays, there are many inconsistencies in the way that alcohol and tobacco on the one hand, and cannabis on the other hand, are regulated. It should be the objective to bring the regulation of these products more fully into convergence. The continuous process to develop an effective regulatory model for cannabis goes hand in hand with the improvement of the regulatory models for alcohol and tobacco.

4. Price Policy and Taxation on Cannabis Products

There is no doubt that a regulated market has an impact on the prices of cannabis products. A big challenge is estimating the possible effects of changes in the prices, the way price control mechanisms will influence the prevalence and the patterns of cannabis use and which effects they will have on the legal and illegal cannabis markets. Determining the most suitable interventions with regard to price control has to do with seeking a balance between conflicting priorities, such as discouraging cannabis use and reducing the size of the illegal cannabis markets.

What are the expected effects of a regulation of the cannabis market on the price of cannabis? The regulation of the cannabis market goes hand in hand with legalizing (decriminalizing) cannabis production and distribution. We may expect that this will lower the price of cannabis. The main reason is that when the production and the distribution of cannabis are taken out of the criminal environment, the risk premium will decline. This means the following. Because of the fact that today the production and distribution of cannabis are illegal, the producers and distributors of cannabis take a risk if they practice these activities. They can get caught, their investments can be forfeited and they can be imprisoned. Thus, they will only want to practice these activities if they receive a sufficiently high compensation for that risk. This is the risk premium. This actually works as an additional production cost and raises the price of cannabis. From the moment that the cannabis market will be legalized and regulated, this risk premium will disappear for the most part and the price of cannabis will go down.

The importance of this price reduction is theoretically hard to determine. It depends amongst other things on the deterrent character of the current repressive system. If the repression is very radical, then the risk premium is high and the price will be able to decrease significantly after the legalization. The reverse is of course the case if there is a tolerance policy. In that case, the risk premium won't be able to decrease markedly, because it is already low.

The main problem of regulation and legalization has to do with the question if, and to what extent, the price reduction of cannabis will increase its consumption. The fear that cannabis consumption will be stimulated as a result of legalization and regulation has become the main argument for many against that legalization and regulation.

Economists use the concept "elasticity" for measuring the effect of price change on demand. The price elasticity of the demand measures to what extent the demand responds to a certain price change. These changes are expressed in percentages in this relative context. For example: If the elasticity is -1, then this means that a price reduction of 1% will have increased the demand by 1%. If the elasticity (in absolute value) is lower than 1, then the demand will rise less than proportionally after a given reduction of the price. For example: if the elasticity is -0.5, then a price reduction of 1% will have increased the demand with only 0.5%. In the case of an elasticity that in absolute value is higher than 1, we have the opposite: the demand responds more than proportionally to a given price change.

So it is important to know the price elasticity of the demand for cannabis in order to be able to estimate what the effect of the price reduction on the use of cannabis will be. A lot of research has been done that econometrically estimates the size of the price elasticity of the demand for cannabis. I need to emphasize the fact that the estimation of the price elasticity of the demand for cannabis is very complex and can lead to large margins of error. The latter has especially to do with the bad quality of the data (both prices and consumption), which in turn is the result of the illegal character of the production and distribution of cannabis.

Summarizing, I can state, from these econometric studies, that the elasticity is situated between 0 and -1, with an average around -0.5. This means that the demand for cannabis really is susceptible to price changes, but this susceptibility remains relatively limited. A decrease in price of cannabis by 10% could raise the demand for cannabis by approximately 5%. I should also emphasize that the elasticity can differ a lot depending on the type of user. The elasticity for a beginning user (initiation) is generally lower (in absolute value) than for a regular user.

Note in this respect that if we assume a price elasticity of -0.5, a decrease in price will decrease the expense of cannabis products (expressed in euros). Expressed in another way: this means that a decrease in the price of cannabis will decrease the cannabis turnover (in euros). This reduces the cannabis market. This is also the main reason why cannabis production and distribution becomes less attractive for criminals after legalization and regulation.

The fact that a drop in price can stimulate (to a lesser degree) the consumption of cannabis, causes a demand for a price policy that has to be established by the regulating government. A government disposes of a series of instruments to limit the decrease in price after legalizing cannabis and thus diminishing the positive effect on consumption or even eliminating it completely.

The state has two main instruments at its disposal to achieve this goal. The first instrument is that the government determines the cannabis prices. If in this case the objective is to prevent a price reduction, it has to impose a minimum price. The second instrument is influencing the prices by levying taxes on the production and/or use of cannabis.

A direct price policy by imposing minimum prices should be prevented. It was the technique formerly used by European authorities in many agricultural markets. There are some well-known disadvantages to this technique. A minimum price raises the profitability of cannabis production and gives strong *"incentives"* to produce a lot. This way, an excess of supply is created that will probably find its way into illegal circulation.

It is advisable to pursue the price policy in an indirect way, in particular by levying taxes. This is also the approach followed by most governments in their price policy with regard to tobacco production and consumption. A state can apply different techniques, for example:

- a *value-added tax, VAT* (a fixed percentage on the sale price, for example 6 or 21 %);
- a *fixed tax on a unit of weight* (for example euros or dollars per gram); this is also called an excise;
- a *fixed tax on the active content* (for example a tax on the relative THC content per unit of weight; so THC percentage per gram);
- a *progressive tax* (by which the tax rate increases in accordance with the potency of the product).

By levying such taxes, the government increases the price of the product and thus can completely or partially counteract the decrease in price that results from legalization and regulation.

The major advantage of taxes in comparison with imposing a minimum price is that the state prevents cannabis production from becoming extra profitable. As stated before, the latter occurs when establishing minimum prices. When a government imposes taxes, it actually makes sure that the extra profit, which is made with a higher price, is pruned away and ends up in the budget.

The latter leads to the second major advantage of taxation. The regulation of the production and the distribution of cannabis, as I present in this book, assumes that the government sets free extra resources in order to regulate and control. A tax generates these resources and also makes it possible for the government to actually fulfil this regulatory and controlling role. This is not possible when a government uses minimum prices as an instrument for the price policy.

5. Drug Policy as Part of a Social Policy

Prevalence of cannabis consumption is often put on a par with prevalence of cannabis-related damage, but the majority of cannabis use is not problematic. Instead of narrowing down the outlook to the reduction of use, a cannabis policy must try to reduce the total damage. The typical cannabis user is far from a criminal and most cannabis consumers are occasional, socially integrated and non-problematic users. If users do excessively use cannabis (abuse or dependence), then there is often a clear link with other personal, psychological, family or social problems. A drug policy that wants to have a meaningful impact on cannabis abuse (and drug abuse in general), has to be *part of a much broader social policy*. Apart from the regulation of cannabis, investments have to be made in order to improve health education, prevention and treatment and a decisive policy concerning poverty, unemployment, social inequality, social exclusion and discrimination must be implemented. If we want to significantly tackle the wider challenges that are coupled with drugs, then legal regulation must go hand in hand with improvements with regard to the current forms of health education, prevention, treatment and recovery, and with the fight against poverty, inequality and social exclusion.

BIBLIOGRAPHY

Americans for Safe Access (2006). *Medical Cannabis Dispensing Collectives and Local Regulation.* Oakland (CA): ASA.

Arana, X. & Montañés Sánchez, V. (2011). Cannabis Cultivation in Spain – the Case of Cannabis Social Clubs (163-177). In: T. Decorte, G. Potter & M. Bouchard (Eds.), *World Wide Weed. Global Trends in Cannabis Cultivation and its Control.* London: Ashgate Publishers.

Barriuso, M. (2005). Propuesta de modelo legal para el cannabis en el estado español. *Eguzkilore, Revista del Instituto Vasco de Criminología,* 19, 151-167.

Barriuso, M. (2011). *Cannabis Social Clubs in Spain. A Normalizing Alternative Underway.* Series on Legislative Reform of Drug Policies, 9.

Bean, Ph. (2010). *Legalising Drugs. Debates and Dilemmas.* Bristol: The Policy Press.

Beauchesne, L. (2007). Une législation des drogues inscrite en promotion de la santé: les conditions. *Criminologie,* 40(1), 135-154.

Bewley-Taylor, D.R. (1999). *The United States and International Drug Control, 1909-1997.* London: Pinter.

Bewley-Taylor, D.R. (2003). Challenging the UN Drug Control Conventions: Problems and Possibilities. *International Journal of Drug Policy,* 14, 171-179.

Bovenkerk, F. (1994). Over de risico's van het legaliseren van de handel in drugs. *Tijdschrift voor Criminologie,* 1, 8-11.

Caputo, M.R. & Ostrom, B.J. (1994). Potential tax revenue from a regulated marijuana market. A meaningful revenue source. *American Journal of Economics and Sociology,* 53(4), 475-490.

Caulkins, J.P., Kilmer, B., MacCoun, R.J., Pacula, R.L. & Reuter, P. (2011). Design considerations for legalizing cannabis: lessons inspired by analysis of California's Proposition 19. *Addiction,* 107(5), 865-871.

Caulkins, J.P. (2018). Hedging bets: applying New Zealand's gambling machine regime to cannabis legalization. *International Journal of Drug Policy,* 53, 113-114.

Chapkiss, W. & Webb, R.J. (2008). *Dying to get high. Marijuana as medicine.* New York: New York University Press.

Chatwin, C. (2007). Multi-level governance: the way forward for European illicit drug policy. *International Journal of Drug Policy,* 18, 494-502.

Cohen, P. (1999). Shifting the main purposes of drug control: from suppression to regulation of use. Reduction of risks as the new focus for drug policy. *International Journal of Drug Policy,* 10, 223-234.

Cussen, M. & Block, W. (2000). Legalize drugs now! An analysis of the benefits of legalized drugs. *American Journal of Economics and Sociology,* 59(3), 525-527.

Decorte, T. (2007). Characteristics of the cannabis market in Belgium (28-38). In: J. Fountain & D.J. Korf (Eds), *Drugs in Society: European Perspectives.* Oxford: Radcliffe Publishing.

Decorte, T. (2008). Domestic cannabis cultivation in Belgium: the (un)intended effects of the national drug policy on the cannabis market (69-86). In: D.J.Korf (Ed.), *Cannabis in Europe: Dynamics in Perception, Policy and Markets.* Lengerich: Pabst.

Decorte, T. (2010). The case for small-scale domestic cannabis cultivation. *International Journal of Drug Policy,* 21(4), 271-275.

Decorte, T., Potter, G. & Bouchard, M. (2011). *World Wide Weed. Global Trends in Cannabis Cultivation and its Control.* London: Ashgate Publishers.

Decorte, T. (2014). *De regulering van cannabis. Lessen uit het verleden en denksporen voor de toekomst.* Thorbeckecolleges. Gandaius–Thorbecke 37. Mechelen: Wolters Kluwer.

Decorte, T., De Grauwe, P. & Tytgat, J. (2014). Het Belgisch cannabisbeleid maakt zijn doelstellingen niet waar. *Panopticon, 35*(2), 151-155.

Decorte, T., De Grauwe, P., & Tytgat, J. (2013). *Cannabis: bis? Pleidooi voor een kritische evaluatie van het Belgische cannabisbeleid.* 18 November 2013.

Decorte, T. (2015). Cannabis Social Clubs in Belgium: Organizational strengths and weaknesses, and threats to the model. *International Journal of Drug Policy, 26,* 122-130.

Decorte, T., & Pardal, M. (2017). Cannabis Social Clubs in Europe: Prospects and Limits. In R. Colson & H. Bergeron (Eds.), *European Drug Policies: The Ways of Reform* (pp. 285-299). New York: Routledge.

Decorte, T., Pardal, M., Queirolo, R., Boidi, M. F., Sanchez, C., & Pares, O. (2017). Regulating Cannabis Social Clubs: a comparative analysis of legal and self-regulatory practices in Spain, Belgium and Uruguay. *International Journal of Drug Policy*(43), 44-56.

Decorte, T., De Grauwe, P., & Tytgat, J. (2016). *Cannabis onder controle: Hoe?* Tielt: Lannoo Campus.

Drucker, E. (1999). Drug Prohibition and Public Health: 25 Years of Evidence. *Public Health Reports, 114,* 14-29.

Dufour, R. (2006). Drugs. Van oorlog naar regulering. *Justitiële Verkenningen, 32*(1), 111-122.

Engelsman, E.L. (2003). Cannabis control: the model of the WHO tobacco control treaty. *International Journal of Drug Policy, 14,* 217-219.

FAGG (2017). FAQ Cannabis. Retrieved December, 07 from https://www.fagg-afmps.be/nl/MENSELIJK_gebruik/

bijzondere_producten/speciaal_gereglementeerde_stoffen/
verdovende_middelen/faq_cannabis

FAGG (2014). Advies van de werkgroep over het gebruik van medicinale cannabis. Commissie voor geneesmiddelen voor menselijk gebruik. Commissie voor kruidengeneesmiddelen voor menselijk gebruik.

Federal Government. (2001). *Beleidsnota van de Federale Regering in verband met de drugproblematiek [Federal Drug Policy Note]*. Brussel: Federale Regering.

Federal Government. (2014). *Federaal regeerakkoord*. Brussel: Federale Regreing.

Fijnaut, C. & De Ruyver, B. (2014). *De derde weg. Een pleidooi voor een evenwichtig cannabisbeleid*. Antwerpen: Intersentia.

Gaoni, Y. & Mechoulam R. (1964). Isolation, structure and partial synthesis of an active constituent of hashish. *Journal of the American Chemical Society* 86(8), 1646-1647.

Gelders, D. & Vander Laenen, F. (2007). 'Mr Police Officer, I thought cannabis was legal' – Introducing new policy regarding cannabis in Belgium: a story of good intentions and Babel. *Drugs: Education, Prevention and Policy*, 14(2), 103-116.

Global Commission on Drug Policy (2011). ~~War~~ on drugs. Retrieved from: www.globalcommissionondrugs.org (on 28 November 2013).

Gray, J.P. (2001). *Why our drug laws have failed and what we can do about it. A judicial indictment of the war on drugs*. Philadelphia: Temple University Press.

Haden, M. (2004). Regulation of illegal drugs: an exploration of public health tools. *International Journal of Drug Policy*, 15, 225-230.

Hall, W. & Lynskey, M. (2009). The challenges in developing a rational cannabis policy. *Current Opinion in Psychiatry*, 22, 258-262.

Hall, W. & Room, R. (2008). Should we criminalize cannabis use? The case against. *The Canadian Journal of Psychiatry*, 53(12), 793-799.

Hayakawa, K., Mishima, K, Fujiwara, M. (2010). Therapeutic potential of non-psychotropic cannabidiol in ischemic stroke. *Pharmaceuticals, 3*(7), 2197-2212.

Hazekamp, A. (2006). An evaluation of the quality of medicinal grade cannabis in the Netherlands. *Cannabinoids, 1*(1), 1-9.

Hughes, C.E. & Stevens, A. (2010). What can we learn from the Portuguese decriminalization of illicit drugs? *British Journal of Criminology, 50*, 999-1022.

Iversen, L. (2004). Cannabis and the law – high time to reform? *European Review, 12*(4), 513-525.

Joossens, L. (2016). *De tabakslobby in België*. Berchem: EPO.

Kilmer, B., Kruithof, K., Pardal, M., Caulkins, J. P., & Rubin, J. (2013). *Multinational overview of cannabis production regimes*. Santa Monica: RAND.

Korf, D. (2002). Dutch coffeeshops and trends in cannabis use. *Addictive Behaviors, 27*, 851-866.

Lap, M. (1993). Een vergunningsstelsel voor cannabis. *Justitiële Verkenningen, 19*(6), 111-119.

Lenton, S. (2000). Cannabis policy and the burden of proof: is it now beyond reasonable doubt that cannabis prohibition is not working? *Drug and Alcohol Review, 19*, 95-100.

Lenton, S. (2003). Policy from a harm reduction perspective. *Current Opinion in Psychiatry, 16*, 271-277.

Leuw, E. & Marshall, I. (1994). *Between prohibition and legalization. The Dutch experiment in drug policy*. Amsterdam/New York: Kugler Publications.

Levine H.G. & Reinarman C. (2004). *Alcohol prohibition and drug prohibition. Lessons from alcohol policy for drug policy*. Amsterdam: Centrum voor Drugsonderzoek.

Levine, H.G. & Reinarman, C. (1998). The transition from prohibition to regulation. In: J. Fish (Ed.), *How to legalize drugs*. Northvale (NJ): Jason Aronson.

MacCoun, R. & Reuter, P. (2001). Evaluating alternative cannabis regimes. *The British Journal of Psychiatry*, 178, 123-128.

Maddox, S. & Williams, S. (1998). Cannabis-related experiences and rate of cultivation: would they change under a policy of decriminalization? *Drugs: Education, Prevention and Policy*, 5(1), 47-58.

McLaren, J., Swift, W., Dillon, P. & Allsop, S. (2008). Cannabis potency and contamination: a review of the literature. *Addiction*, 103, 1100-1109.

Miron, J.A. (2004). *Drug war crimes. The consequences of prohibition*. Oakland, California: The Independent Institute.

Mishan, E.J. (2001). The staggering costs of drug criminalization. *Economic Affairs*, 37-41.

Nicholson, T. (1992). The primary prevention of illicit drug problems: an argument for decriminalisation and legalization. *The Journal of Primary Prevention*, 12(4), 275-288.

Ogilvie, D., Gruer, L. & Haw, S. (2005). Young people's access to tobacco, alcohol and other drugs. *British Medical Journal*, 331, 393-396.

Pacula, R. & Lundberg, R. (2014). Why Changes in Price Matters When Thinking about Marihuana Policy: A Review of the Literature on the Elasticity of Demand. *Public Health Reviews*, 35(2).

Pardal, M. (2016). Cannabis Social Clubs in Belgium: growing in a legal haze? In: J. de Maillard, A. Groenmeyer, P. Ponsaers, J. Shapland & F. Viannello (Eds.), *Crime and order, criminal justice experiences and desistance*. GERN Research Paper Series, 4, 13-30. Antwerpen: Maklu.

Pardal, M. (2016). Cannabis social clubs through the lens of the drug user movement. *Tijdschrift over Cultuur en Criminaliteit*, (6)2, 47-58.

Pardal, M. (2018). The Belgian Cannabis Social Club landscape. *Drugs & Alcohol Today*. 18(2).

Pardal, M., & Tieberghien, J. (2017). An analysis of media framing of and by Cannabis Social Clubs in Belgium: making the news? *Drugs: Education, Prevention and Policy.* 24(4), 348-358.

Pardal, M. (2018). An analysis of Belgian Cannabis Social Clubs' supply practices: A shapeshifting model?, *International Journal of Drug Policy,* 57, 32-41.

Pardal, M. (2018). "The difference is in the tomato at the end": understanding the motivations and practices of cannabis growers operating within Belgian Cannabis Social Clubs. *International Journal of Drug Policy,* 56, 21-29.

Pudney, S. (2010). Drugs policy: what should we do about cannabis? *Economic Policy,* 165-211.

Raschke, P. & Kalke, J. (1999). Cannabis in pharmacies: a proposal from Germany on how to separate the drug markets. *International Journal on Drug Policy,* 10, 309-311.

Rasmussen, D.W. & Benson, B.L. (1994). *The economic anatomy of a drug war.* Lanham, Maryland: Rowman and Littlefield Publishers.

Reinarman, C. (2009). Cannabis policies and user practices: market separation, price, potency, and accessibility in Amsterdam and San Francisco. *International Journal of Drug Policy,* 20, 28-37.

Reuband, K.H. (1998). Drug policies and drug prevalence: the role of demand and supply. *European Journal on Criminal Policy and Research,* 6, 321-336.

Ritter, A. & Cameron, J. (2006). A review of the efficacy and effectiveness of harm reduction strategies for alcohol, tobacco and illicit drugs. *Drug and Alcohol Review,* 25, 611-624.

Roberts, M., Bewley-Taylor, D. & Trace, M. (2005). *Facing the future: the challenge for national & international drug policy.* The Beckley Foundation Drug Policy Programme, Report nr. 6.

Robinson, M.B. & Scherlen, R.G. (2007). *Lies, damned lies and drug war statistics.* Albany: State University of New York Press.

Single, E. (1999). Options for cannabis reform. *International Journal of Drug Policy*, 10, 281-290.

Solomon, R., Single, E. & Erickson, P. (1983). Legal Considerations in Canadian Cannabis Policy. *Canadian Public Policy/Analyse de Politiques*, 9(4), 419-433.

Teurlings, M. & Cohen, P. (2005). Het regelen van de 'achterdeur' van coffeeshops. Onderzoek naar juridische belemmeringen. *Nederlands Juristenblad*, 5, 298-302.

Tieberghien, J. (2017). *Change or continuity in drug policy: the roles of science, media, and interest groups*. New York: Routledge.

Transform Drug Policy Foundation (2007). *After the war on drugs. Tools for the debate*. Bristol: Transform.

Transform Drug Policy Foundation (2009). *After the War on Drugs: Blueprint for Regulation*. Bristol: Transform.

Transform Drug Policy Foundation (2013). *How to regulate cannabis. A practical guide*. Bristol: Transform.

Tullis, L. (1995). *Unintended consequences. Illegal drugs and drug policies in nine countries*. Boulder/London: Lynne Rienner Publishers.

van der Veen, H.T. (2009). Regulation in spite of prohibition. The control of cannabis distribution in Amsterdam. *Cultural Critique*, 71, 129-147.

Vander Laenen, F. (2004). De nieuwe Ministeriële Omzendbrief voor druggebruikers. Het vervolgingsbeleid laat er zich niet door leiden. *Panopticon*, 25(5), 9-29.

Vander Laenen, F., De Ruyver, B., Christiaens, J. & Lievens, D. (2011). *Drugs in cijfers III. Onderzoek naar de overheidsuitgaven voor het drugsbeleid in België*. Gent: Academia Press.

van Ooyen, M.M.J., Bieleman, B. & Korf, D.J. (2013). *Het besloten club- en het ingezetenencriterium voor coffeeshops. Evaluatie van de implementatie en de uitkomsten in de periode mei-november 2012. Tussenrapportage*. Cahier 2013-2. Den Haag: WODC.

Wilkins, C. & Casswell, S. (2002). The cannabis black market and the case for the legalisation of cannabis in New Zealand. *Social Policy Journal of New Zealand*, 18, 31-430.

Wilkins, C. (2018). A "not-for-profit" regulatory model for legal recreational cannabis: insights from the regulation of gaming machine gambling in New Zealand. *International Journal of Drug Policy*, 53, 115-122.

Wodak, A. (2002). Cannabis control: costs outweigh the benefits. *British Medical Journal*, 324, 105-324.

Wodak, A. & Cooney, A. (2004). Should cannabis be taxed and regulated? *Drug and Alcohol Review*, 23, 139-141.

Wouters, M. & Korf, D.J. (2009). Access to licensed cannabis supply and the separation of markets policy in the Netherlands. *Journal of Drug Issues*, 39(3), 627-652.

ABOUT THE AUTHOR

Tom Decorte is professor of Criminology at Ghent University (Belgium) where he is the director of the Institute for Social Drug research (ISD). He has co-founded the *Global Cannabis Cultivation Research Consortium* (GCCRC) and is currently trustee of the Board of the *European Society for Social Drug research* (ESSD) and of the *International Society for the Study of Drug Policy* (ISSDP). Tom Decorte has published widely on patterns of substance use, on the supply side of cannabis markets, and on the development and implementation of local monitoring systems of drug policies.